What does P

Which w
legitim
it apparently doesn't exist?

. . .

If "migrants" are people who move from place
to place, what do you call people
who stay in one place?

. . .

The answers to these and many more
linguistic puzzles lie within *The Dictionary of
Highly Unusual Words*—a highly unusual
reference for anyone who loves words!

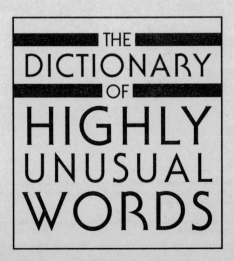

THE
DICTIONARY
OF
HIGHLY
UNUSUAL
WORDS

THE
DICTIONARY
OF
HIGHLY
UNUSUAL
WORDS

IRWIN M. BERENT
and ROD L. EVANS

BERKLEY BOOKS, NEW YORK

THE DICTIONARY OF HIGHLY UNUSUAL WORDS

A Berkley Book / published by arrangement with
the authors

PRINTING HISTORY
Berkley edition / January 1997

The Putnam Berkley World Wide Web site address is
http://www.berkley.com/berkley

ISBN: 0-425-15606-0

BERKLEY®
Berkley Books are published by The Berkley Publishing Group,
200 Madison Avenue, New York, New York 10016.
BERKLEY and the "B" design are trademarks
belonging to Berkley Publishing Corporation.

PRINTED IN THE UNITED STATES OF AMERICA

10 9 8 7 6 5 4 3 2 1

A

a It is a fact, according to the *American Heritage Word Frequency Book* (New York: American Heritage, 1971), that you are looking at a word that is one of the ten most commonly used words in the English language. And can you guess what the others are?

à la king The "à la king" of chicken à la king has, in fact, nothing to do with royalty and more correctly should be "à la *keene*," for the dish was named after either J. R. Keene or his son, Foxhall Keene.

Aaaahtamad Have you ever seen a word with four *a*'s in a row and six *a*'s all together? Well, now you have! The word pertains to an unidentified town in Palestine.

aalii This may seem to denote the sound of people cheering for Muhammad Ali. Actually, it's a Hawaiian word for a small tree *(Dodonaea viscosa)* valued for its hard, dark wood.

abacot This word was originally "bicocket," but because of a misprint the misspelling gained a footing in dictionaries. The word "bicocket," which denoted a peaked cap or head-dress, was once misprinted "abococket." Slowly, writers

---

copied the error, soon refining the word to "abococke" and finally "abacot."

abandon A music group in full gear.

Aberuthven You might never have guessed that the name of this place in the British Isles is pronounced "aberiven."

ABLISS This may sound like a word for "having great happiness." Actually, though, it's an acronym for the Association of British Library and Information Science Schools. After all, what could make one more abliss than working in a library?

abracadabras This is one of the longest words using only the *a* for its vowel.

abstemious This word has all five vowels, each appearing only once, in alphabetical order! The word means "practicing moderation or temperance."

abstentious This word has all five vowels, each appearing only once, in alphabetical order! The word means "characterized by abstinence."

Abyssinia And I'll be seeing *you!*

accentuation Scramble the letters of this word and the appropriate result is "I can cut a tone."

Accident Wonder how Accident, Maryland, got its name? Perhaps by accident!

Accidentals What else would you call people who live in Accident, Maryland? In fact, that *is* precisely what the residents call themselves!

accommodating And I come a-courting?

accomplice There's a great deal of complicity in this word. The next time you speak of "an accomplice," consider that at

---

2

one time people spoke of "a complice," for the word was originally two words, "a complice"—that is, a person who is in complicity with another. Apparently the article "a," in complicity with "complice," fused itself, and then added another *c* to complete the deception.

accordion   The "cord" in the name of this musical instrument does not relate directly to chords. In fact, it is related to "accord," since the music has harmony, or accord, and is "to the heart," from Latin *ad,* meaning "to," and *cor, cordis,* meaning "heart," as in "*card*iac."

Aceeeffghhiillmmnnoorrssstuv   What twisted logic did the German novelist Christoffel von Grimmelshausen use when he came up with this pseudonym? Actually, it isn't as twisted as it might appear. He simply rearranged all the letters of his name—in alphabetical order!

acetylsalicylic   This is the name of an acid—a drug—that most people use quite often (yes, it's true, we are a nation of acidheads). Fortunately, though, this drug is legal; we don't even need a prescription to buy it. But this word has gone out of favor for obvious reasons—it's hard to pronounce. It seems that people got tired of asking for acetylsalicylic acid. And when a company came up with a short, easy-to-pronounce brand name for it, people preferred using that name. In fact, the new name became so popular that the brand name, which once was the company's legal trademark, fell into the public domain. The name of the product was Aspirin. Today it's just aspirin.

acheilous   This word has all the vowels, each appearing only once, in alphabetical order! The word means "having no lips."

acoustic   If you want to play pool, you've got to have acoustic!

---

actors   Scramble the letters of this word and the appropriate result is "costar"!

adenochondrosarcoma   This is one of the longest words beginning and ending with *a*.

adinida   This word is a palindrome; it reads the same way backward and forward. "Adinida" is the name of a primitive protozoan.

Admiral   This word could have been shorter than it is. The word comes from the title of Abu Bekr, *amir-al-muninin*, "commander of the faithful." But if "admiral" were shortened only to "amiral," it would mean roughly "commander of the." So how come the word isn't simply "amir" (commander)?

admirer   One way to get married is to get mixed up with an admirer. An easier way to get "married" is to mix up the letters in the word "admirer."

admonition   Scramble the letters of "admonition" and you have "domination."

adultery   Contrary to what some of you may think—or wish—this word does not mean "what adults do." The "adult" in "adultery" is, in fact, purely coincidental. For "adultery" is related to "adulterate" (to corrupt, to make impure). The word "adult," however, is related to "*adol*escent" (one who has grown up). Perhaps it would be less confusing if adults were called "adolts."

advertisements   Scramble the letters of this word and the appropriate result is "items at venders"!

Aeaea   This is a classic all-vowel word! It was the name of a small island off the coast of Italy.

affable   Affable and half a cow—a cowbull, that is!

4

affectionately This is probably the shortest English word in which you can find the letters that constitute "fifty-one."

aftercataracts If you're left-handed and you can type, this may be one of your favorite words. For "aftercataracts" is one of the longest words containing only letters that are typed with the left hand (*qwert, asdf,* and *zxcv*).

AGREE This is an acronym for NASA's Advanced Ground Receiving Equipment Experiment.

AINDT No, this ain't a misspelling of "ain't." It's an acronym for the Australian Institute for Non-Destructive Testing!

Ajaja ajaja No matter how you look at this two-word scientific name for the roseate spoonbill, it says the same thing. Read it backward and see!

alarms The octopus seems to be alarms—and all legs?

alarum This isn't exactly a misspelling of "alarm." It's the British spelling of the word.

Albany This city name is also a part-abbreviation, part-acronym for the following: Adjustment of Large Blocks with *any* number of photos, points, and images, using *any* photogrammetric measuring instrument and on *any* computer. There's nothing like a clear abbreviation!

Albuquerque This place-name could have been "Albu*r*querque," for the city was named after the viceroy of New Spain, the Duke of Albur*querque. It seems that there was some confusion with the better-known Alfonso Albuquerque (1453–1515), the Portuguese viceroy of the Portuguese Indies, who was not blessed with the extra *r.*

ALERT This is the appropriate acronym for the American Lifesaving Emergency Response Team.

alevin This is not a phonetic spelling of "eleven" but the word for a young fish, especially a newly hatched salmon. It comes from the Old French *alever*, meaning "to lift up, or rear, [offspring]."

algorithm An algorithm has nothing to do with rhythm. Nor does its origin have anything to do with a*rithm*etic. In fact, the word was originally spelled "algorism." Yet it wasn't an ism, either. Ultimately the word came from the name of its inventor, Arab mathematician Mohammed ibn-Musa al-Khwarizmi (780–ca. 850). So why isn't it called an alkhwarizmi—sounds much more rhythmic, doesn't it? By the way, "algorism" became "algorithm" partly because of its association with the word "arithmetic."

Alicel The Oregon place-name comes from Alice L. The *L* stands for Ladd.

aliform This sounds like a word for Ali's boxing style. Actually it means "wing-shaped." The "al" part is related in origin to "aisle"—at one time, a "wing," or side, of a church.

alligator This is actually a two-word fusion. It comes from the Spanish phrase *el lagarto,* meaning simply "the lizard." So now you know what an alligator is—a lizard!

allonym This isn't the name of an organization for those affected by alcoholism. Rather it is the word for a name assumed by an author but actually belonging to another person. Hence, if you're told that the authors of this book are George Washington and Thomas Jefferson, you should be reasonably confident that either we are using allonyms or someone is playing a dastardly joke on you. The "all" part of this word is related in origin to "else," which is from the Greek *allos,* meaning "other" or "different." The "onym" part is found also in, for example, "an*onym*ous" (having no name).

6

almoner   This sounds like the word for someone who likes or grows almonds. Actually it denotes one who distributes charitable gifts—an almsgiver, that is.

ALOFT   This is the appropriate acronym for the U.S. Navy's Airborne Light/Optical Fiber Technology.

alphabetically   Scramble the letters of this word and you get "I play all the ABC."

alterations   Scramble the letters of this word and you get "neat tailors."

alula   This word is a palindrome; it reads the same way backward and forward. An alula is the false wing of a bird.

aluminium   This isn't exactly a misspelling of "aluminum." It's the British spelling of the word.

amadelphous   This may appear to pertain to a mad elf, but it actually means "gregarious" or "sociable." It originates from the Greek *hama* (together with) and *adelphos,* (brotherly), as in Philadelphia, the City of Brotherly Love.

amathophobia   You might think that amathophobia is an irrational fear of math. In fact, it is a fear of dust. It comes from the Greek *amathos* (sand).

ambidextrously   This is one of the longest English words with no repeated letters.

amiable   This word is "pregnant" with triplets: "am," "I," and "able."

Amish   These people might have been called Ammonish, since the name was taken from Jacob Ammon.

amok   This is one of the few words that can be split in such a way as to suggest the opposite meaning of the original word.

"Amok" can be split to form "am OK," yet one who is OK is usually *not* amok!

Amotherby   This town in Britain is pronounced "Amerby."

ampulaceous   This word may appear to pertain to something that is ample to an extreme. In fact, it means "shaped like a flask or bladder."

amurca   This may appear to be a misspelling of "America." In fact, it is the name of the sediment in olive oil.

an aisle   Scramble the letters of this phrase and the appropriate result will be "is a lane."

ana   This means "a collection of amusing or entertaining stories about some person or place." Its more common cousin is found at the end of other words, as in "Americ*ana*."

anathema   Remove a few letters from this word for "curse" and then scramble the rest. The appropriate result is "hate."

Anchorage   The name of this city in Alaska could have been Knik Anchorage or at least Knik. Before the town was officially established in 1914, its name was Knik Anchorage. "Knik" probably originated from an Eskimo word for "fire." An anchorage, of course, is a harbor or port. Thus, the part of the original name that *described* the port—that gave to the town a distinctive name—was dropped.

ANCIRS   This is not a misspelling of "answers." It is, in fact, a somewhat appropriate acronym for Automatic News Clipping, Indexing, and Retrieval System. One wonders how reliable such a service might be, if it can't even spell "answers" correctly!

angary   This is not a leisurely phonetic spelling of "angry." Rather it is a term of international law pertaining to the right of a belligerent to seize, use, or destroy the property of neutrals. Kind of makes you angary, doesn't it?

angelicals This remarkable word is built on nine other real words: "a," "an," "ang," "ange," "angel," "angeli," "angelic," "angelica," and "angelical."

angered Scramble the letters of this word and the appropriate result is "enraged."

Angleland Not the land of angles, like triangles, but the original word from which "England" came. In other words, the land of the Anglo-Saxons, or the Angles and the Saxons.

animative Actually a very nutritious word. Ignore the last letter of this word, read the remainder in reverse, and what do you get? "Vitamin A"!

animosity Rid yourself of animosity and you'll have amity; remove a few letters from "animosity" and you'll have "amity."

Annapolitans The residents of Annapolis, Maryland, do not call themselves Annapolisians; they call themselves Annapolitans! And why not? People living in a metropolis are metropolitans.

anserine This word may appear to mean "pertaining to answering." In fact, it means "pertaining to geese," or "silly." The word is related to the Greek *anser* (goose).

antagonist Scramble the letters of "antagonist" and you have "stagnation."

Antass Wouldn't this be a great name for a city in Idaho? Antass, ID—antacid!

antelope Insect's secret marriage?

———

9

antenna array This term for a kind of radio antenna is one of those rare phrases containing three consecutive pairs of like letters.

anthem This word is the product of a distortion of the original Latin word "antiphona," literally meaning "opposite sounding"—in other words, "responding to the sound."

anticonstitutionnnellement This is perhaps the longest word in the French language. It means "anticonstitutionally."

antonym One boy, one girl, and two ants came to a picnic. Before long, there was an ant on her and an antonym!

apolaustic This word may appear to mean "given to applauding." In fact, it means "devoted to pleasure."

APPALLING This apt but ironic acronym warning was coined by usage expert Theodore Bernstein. It stands for Acronym Production, Particularly At Lavish Levels, Is No Good!

apron Have you ever worn a napron? An apron was originally called a "napron." But "a napron" sounds a lot like "an apron," so people began to think that the word for a napron was "apron."

aprosexia This word actually has nothing to do with sex. It means "an inability to concentrate." "Pros" and "ex" are separate roots of this word.

aqueous This word has four vowels in a row.

archaic We've got our ice cream, but where's archaic?

archcharlatans This is one of the longest words using only the *a* as its vowel.

Arnold   Amazingly, this name can be scrambled into five other first names: Landor, Nordal, Roland, Roldan, and Ronald.

arrest   After several hours of work, he could use arrest!

arsenious   This word has all the vowels, each appearing only once, in alphabetical order. The word means "of, relating to, or containing arsenic."

ARTEMIS   This is the acronym for the Administrative Real Time Express Mortgage and Investment System.

Asakasa   This word is a palindrome; it reads the same way backward and forward. It is the name of a Buddhist pagoda in Tokyo.

aspersion   Scramble the letters of this word and the appropriate result is "no praise."

aspirate   This remarkable word is built on seven other real words: "a," "as," "asp," "aspi," "aspir," "aspira," and "aspirat."

aspiration   The taking of aspirin for an ailment?

aspire   Perhaps nothing makes people aspire more than giving them praise. Simply scramble the letters in "aspire" and you'll have "praise." Be careful though, for if you scramble "praised," you might get "despair."

ASSASSIN   This, believe it or not, is an acronym for the Agricultural System for Storage And Subsequent Selection of Information.

assess   A female donkey?

Associated Press   Remove a few letters from this phrase and then scramble the rest. The appropriate result is "editor's space."

asssse   Now *that's* a royal pain! This four *s*'s-in-a-row word is actually an old spelling of "ashes."

———

astronomers   Scramble the letters of this word and you get "moon starers."

auburn   Because the "burn" part of this word resembles "brown," it has taken on the meaning of "brown." Yet were we to spell the word in its more nearly original form, we would discover that its true roots were not brown. The Middle French version of this word was spelled "alborne." And it is no coincidence that the "alb" part of this word is also found in "albino," for the original meaning of both those words was indeed not "brown" but "white."

Auchindachie   You might never have guessed that this British place-name is pronounced "ochinachi."

Auraria   Just about everyone has heard of the Denver Nuggets basketball team. The reason they're called the Nuggets is that Denver was a gold-mining center. Have you ever daydreamed about how nice it would be if the city were named Golden instead of Denver? Then the Denver Nuggets would be, appropriately, the Golden Nuggets! (Of course, you have probably never had such a daydream, since you probably have other things to think about—we hope. But for the sake of our story, *pretend* that this is important to you.) Well, it turns out that, before the name of the city was changed in 1859 (to honor James W. Denver, a former governor of the territory), it was called Auraria. And what do you suppose "auraria" means in Latin? "Golden"!

austinclarki   This is part of the formal scientific name for an Eocene pelecypod, the *Nucula austinclarki*. You might ask, "So what?" But this name is unusual, for it is named after a man. You might still ask, "So what? Quite a number of things are named after persons." But this name is unusual because it contains the full name of that person: Austin Clark.

avenue   A more "sophisticated" use of this word: "I avenue baby-sitter."

B

bacteria The back of the cafeteria?

Baires Some people in Buenos Aires think the name of their city is too long, so they call it simply "Baires." Actually, they should be grateful that the official name given by the Spanish settlers in 1535 is no longer used. That name is as follows: Ciudad de la Santísima Trinidad y puerto de nuestra señora la virgen Maria de los buenos aires (City of the Most Holy Trinity and Port of Our Lady the Virgin Mary of Good Winds).

Bakelite This brand name is actually named for Leo Hendrik Baekeland. So the word could have been Baekelandite.

Bakester This is the original name from which the surname Baxter came. Like many words that end in "ster," this word denoted a female worker. The male, in this case, was called a baker; the female was called a bakester, just as Webber and Webster were, respectively, a male and a female weaver of cloth.

Ballground This word represents perhaps the largest "ballground" in the world, a "ballground" as big as a city. Actually,

Ballground is the name of a city in Mississippi. Apparently the area contained Indian burial grounds that resembled large balls.

Balquhidder   This British place-name is pronounced "bal-widder."

bandy   The idea of "bandying something about" actually originates from a sixteenth-century Irish precursor of ice hockey known as bandy, in which a ball was—you guessed it—hit back and forth.

bang   This word comes from the sound of a bang; it's onomatopoeic.

bangs   The tail of this word has been lost, literally. For just as "ponytail" and "pigtail" denote hairstyles named for animals' tails, the word "bang" originates from "bang*tail*"—a short-tailed horse.

banoney   If this word looks a little bit like "baloney," there is good reason. One might wonder, in fact, why the baloney (or bologna) we eat is not called "banoney," for the city of Bologna, Italy, where the sausages were first made, was known in the fourth century B.C. as Bononia. Only much later was the *n* changed to *l*. No baloney!

banquet   Savings and loan dry. Banquet!

barefaced   Except for the *r,* this nine-letter word contains only the first six letters of the alphabet.

barking   This word is "pregnant" with twins: "bar" and "king."

bartender   Scramble the letters of this word and you'll see how bartenders view their work: "beer 'nd art."

---

basalt   The only indication that this is the word for a type of rock (and by the way, it has nothing to do with salt) is in the last two letters, *l* and *t*. Those letters are all that remain of the original Greek word *lithos,* meaning "stone"—as in "monolith," literally "a single stone." For "basalt" originated with the Greek phrase, *basanites lithos,* meaning touchstone. So why not call it "basalith"?

bassinet   The goal of a fisherman?

bayonets   Remove a few letters from this word and scramble the rest. The appropriate result is "Stab one!"

Bearwardcote   This British place-name is pronounced "baracut."

bedeafed   "Bedeafed" is a piano word—that is, a word that is composed entirely of letters representing notes on the piano: *a, b, d, e, f,* and *g.* Only the *c* is missing.

BEDECKED   Write this word in full capital letters, place a mirror above the word and perpendicular to the paper, and what do you get? "BEDECKED!"

bedevil   This word is "pregnant" with twins: "bed" and "evil."

before   To transform into quadruplets?

begonia   This plant is named for botanist Michel Bégon. So perhaps it should be "bégonia."

behoove   To have hooves?

Beijing   Notice anything unusual about this word? It contains three consecutive dotted letters, a rarity.

---

belfry   There was no bell in the earliest belfry. True, a belfry is the part of a tower where the bell hangs, but the "bel" in this word has nothing to do with bells. "Belfry" comes from the Old French *berfrei*, which, roughly translated, means "peace-protector." After all, a fort, with its defensive tower and belfry, is indeed a peace-protector.

belligerents   Scramble this word, and it still amounts to a "rebelling set."

benign   If you add 12 to 5, and then subtract 8, the total will benign!

Beukel   What would we have put on our hamburgers had it not been for William Beukel (or Beukelz)? For certain, we would not be putting pickles on them. Indeed, we'd probably never be in a pickle were it not for Mr. Beukel, for it was from Beukel that the pickle got its name.

BICEPS   Here's an acronym with some muscle: the Basic Industrial Control Engineering Programming System.

bicycle   This word is a hybrid, a combination of root words from two different languages. The "bi" prefix is Latin, but "cycle" is of Greek origin.

Big Ben   The famous clock (actually, the bell) could have been called "Big Sir Benjamin Hall," since he was the Ben for whom it was named.

bigamist   When it's-a very foggy in Italy, we like-a to say that there's a bigamist?

bigamy   The opposite of a pygmy?

Biguh   Wouldn't this be a great name for a city in Maine? Biguh, ME—bigamy!

bilk   When you say that someone bilked you out of your money, you're using an expression that originated in cribbage. The term refers to the practice of spoiling, or "balking," an opponent.

Bison bison bison   This is the formal name of the American bison. You didn't realize that animals had full names, did you?

bitternesses   This remarkable word is built on ten other real words: "bi," "bit," "bitt," "bitte," "bitter," "bittern," "bitterne," "bitternes," "bitterness," and "bitternesse."

black   Let's stop thinking that black Americans created black magic. If you are to blame anyone for black magic, blame it on corpses. Yes, corpses! Long ago, "necromancy" was the name of the practice of divining, or conjuring, with corpses. *Necro* is from *nekros,* meaning "corpse," as in "necrology," another word for "obituary." The "necro" was mistaken for "nigro" ("black"), and the rest is history.

bleat   This word comes from the sound of a sheep's bleating; it's onomatopoeic.

blessing   Scramble the letters in "blessing" and you have "glibness."

blindfold   Although a blindfold is often a folded cloth tied over the eyes, there is no "fold" in "blindfold." The word originates from *blindfelle,* meaning "to strike blind." The *felle* part is related to "fell" in the sense that to "fell" a tree means to strike it. You might wonder why "blindfold" isn't spelled "blindfeld."

blizzard   In the early 1800s this was a shooting term, denoting a volley of shots. Later in the nineteenth century the word was used to describe a flurry of punches in boxing.

---

blossoms Another word for "blossoms" is inside this word. It's "blooms."

blue Virtually the same word that means "blue" in Romanian means "whitish" in Low Latin; and virtually the same word that means "blue" in Lithuanian means "black" in Greek.

boardinghouse Remove a few letters from this word and scramble the rest. The appropriate result is "hunger aid."

bobble This word is noteworthy for one reason: it can be construed as a fairly long computer word—that is, when it's written in full block-style capital letters and turned upside down. It forms computer-style numbers: BOBBLE turned upside down becomes 378808. _____

bobwhite This word comes from the sound that this genus of quail makes; it's onomatopoeic.

bogus "Bogus" may be bogus: the word probably comes from "borghese," since it is Mr. Borghese for whom the word was named.

boldface Except for the *o,* this eight-letter word contains only the first six letters of the alphabet!

bookkeeper This is perhaps the only non-hyphenated word in the English language that contains three consecutive pairs of letters.

boom This word comes from the sound of a boom; it's onomatopoeic.

borsht If you don't care for borsht, just shake it up—scramble it, that is—and see what happens: broths.

----

bossship   Three *s*'s in a row.

bowlegged   This word is "pregnant" with twins: "bowl" and "egged."

boysenberry   Why would anyone want to call a fruit a boysenberry? Well, apparently Rudolph Boysen, who named this berry, had some reason for calling it that. Wonder what it was?

Braggadocio   Would you believe that this is the name of a community in Missouri?

Bredon   This is the name of a hill in Leicestershire, England. Literally, it is Welsh *bre,* meaning "hill" and Old English *don,* meaning "hill." So this place is literally "hill hill." Right? Well, not quite. For you see, its *full* name is not Bredon; it's Bredon on the Hill!

Breuckelen   This is what Brooklyn, New York, could have been called! For Breuckelen is the name of a village in Holland for which the borough of New York City was named.

brid   No, this is not a misspelling of "bird." It is, rather, a very old spelling of "bird." By the year 1200, "brid" was the accepted spelling of the name of the winged creature. Yet by the linguistic process known as metathesis, the *r* and *i* sounds gradually were inverted, so that by 1353, "brid" had become "bird." And brids no longer flew.

Bromesberrow   This British place-name has had 161 different spellings since the tenth century.

Bronx   This borough of New York City could have been called "Bronck," as it was named after Jonas Bronck.

brush   Scramble the letters of this word and you get "shrub."

Brylcreem   This name for a hair dressing by Beecham Group is a combination of "brilliantine" and "cream," with stylized spelling. Unlike the brilliantine, oils, and gums in use when Brylcreem was first marketed in 1928, Brylcreem contained no gum or starch.

bubble   This word comes from the sound of a bubble; it's onomatopoeic.

bulldoze   Is this a sleeping animal?

bulletin   Gun clean? Yes. Gun cocked? Yes. Bulletin? No!

bulwark   Opposite of cow play?

bump   This word comes from the sound of something getting bumped; it's onomatopoeic.

buoyant   Some insects are so small that one wonders how entomologists can tell the girl ant from the buoyant!

burp   This word comes from the sound of a burp; it's onomatopoeic.

butterfly   Scramble the letters of this word and you get what butterflies do: "flutter by."

butteriness   This word is built on eight other real words: "bu," "but," "butt," "butte," "butter," "butteri," "butterin," "butterine," and "butterines."

C

cabaret Lineup of taxis?

cabbaged "Cabbaged" is a piano word—that is, a word composed entirely of letters representing the notes in a musical octave: *a, b, c, d, e,* and *g.* Only the *f* is missing. Now, we know that some of you are saying, "They made that word up! Who ever heard of something being cabbaged? What does that mean—to adorn with cabbage heads?" First, we are hurt that you would think we would invent a word just so that we could present a piano word. And second, "cabbaged" is the past tense of "cabbage," a verb used as early as 1712 to mean "steal" or "filch." Satisfied?

cabotage This may sound like the name of a cabbagelike plant. In fact, it means "trade or shipping along a coast."

cacophony In an August 1946 poll taken by the National Association of Teachers of Speech, this word ranked among the ten worst-sounding words in the English language.

caesious This is one of the shortest English words that has all the vowels, each appearing only once, in alphabetical order. The word means "blue with a tinge of green."

---

calenture This may appear to mean "pertaining to calendars." In fact, it denotes a fever caused by heat, or it can mean "passion, ardor, zeal."

Calexico Guess what border this California city is located on. The Mexican border, of course!

Calneva Calneva is located along the California–Nevada border. Where else!

Calzona Calzona is located along the California–Arizona border!

Cambridge The British city of Cambridge has nothing to do with any bridge. But since *cambo-rit-um* (the ford in the crooked river) sounded like "cambridge," that's what it became.

camel The camel that gave us the camel's-hair brush is actually no camel at all. The brush was originally made from squirrel hair. Camel—actually Kemel—was the name of a German artist who used the brushes.

camelot A parking lot for camels?

cameralistics This may sound like a word for the study of camera angles or a word meaning "highly realistic photographs" (as opposed to unrealistic photographs?) In fact, it is the science of public finance.

candidate This word has three consecutive words within it: "can," "did," and "ate."

candy A candy is good, but personally, I prefer a *fresh e* to a canned one!

cantaloupe If we cantaloupe, I guess we'll have to have a full-blown wedding ceremony.

---

cantilever   Cantilever? No! I'll never leave her!

CAPABLE   This is an acronym for Controls And Panel Arrangement By Logical Evaluation.

capsize   A little smaller than your hat size?

captation   This word does not refer to the act of putting a head on a person—that is, the opposite of "decapitation." Rather it denotes an attempt to earn favorable attention, especially artfully. It is related to "captivation."

carnificial   This may sound like a carnival official. In fact, it means "of or relating to an executioner or butcher."

Cardinalis cardinalis cardinalis   This is the scientific name of the bird: cardinal!

caricature   A caricature reveals something about the character of its subject. So surely this word is a variation of the word "character." But no! In fact, the word originates from the Italian *caricatura,* meaning "distortion." That word, in turn, comes from the verb *caricare,* "to load." The idea, then, is that caricatures are loaded, in the sense of being less than accurate.

caricaturist   Remove a few letters from this word and scramble the rest. The appropriate result is "caustic art."

Carona   This is not a misspelling of "corona." It is the name of a town in Kansas that lost its "b." The place was originally named Carbona because of the local coal mines.

Carrawburgh   This British place-name is pronounced "carrabruff."

Carson   The "Carson" in Carson City, Nevada, is not what it appears to be. It looks like someone's surname, such as Johnny Carson. In fact, though, it is a combination of parts of the names of two Nevada businessmen, Frank *Car*ter and Simon Peder*son*.

cartoon   Why is a cartoon a "cartoon" and not a "carton"? Perhaps "cartoon" sounds funnier than "carton." Yet the word "cartoon" comes from the French word *carton,* which originally meant "cardboard" and was later extended to mean "a drawing sketched on cardboard." Of course, in English we still have "cardboard cartons," but the funnies are now "cartoons."

cartoonist   Remove a few letters from this word, and the appropriate result is "artist."

casemate   One's lawyer?

cashew   Why isn't a cashew "an acashew"? A confusing question, isn't it? Yet "cashew" comes from the French "acajou." So, again, why isn't a cashew "an acashew"?

castanet   Castanet and see what you catch!

caste   Scramble this word, and it still amounts to "a sect."

catchphrase   This word has made a name for itself by having six—count 'em, six—consonants in a row.

Catholic   Someone who loves—that is, who is addicted to—cats?

cauterize   She never noticed him until one day he cauterize. It was love at first sight!

cellophane   There was a time when, strictly speaking, we could not have legitimately written this word in lowercase.

24

For the word was originally a company's registered trademark, a brand name, and therefore required a capital letter and, sometimes, a trademark symbol: Cellophane™.

celluloid This word, like "cellophane," was originally a brand name: Celluloid™.

certifying You can transpose the first and third letters of this word and come up with another word, "rectifying."

chainlets Two other words are hidden in this word. Take the first letter and then every other letter, and you'll get "canes." Now make another word out of what remains by taking every other letter, starting with the *h*: "hilt."

champagne Phony window glass?

Chang This is an extraordinarily ordinary word. And it is precisely because it is such an ordinary word that we present it to you. In fact, Chang is the most common surname in the world; about 75 million persons have it.

charette This may appear to be the name of a kind of cigarette. In fact, it denotes a final intensive effort to finish an architecture design project before the deadline. The word comes from the French *charrette* (the cart used to transport drawings).

charitableness Scramble the letters of this word and you get "I can bless earth."

chatter This word comes from the sound of chatter; it's onomatopoeic.

CHECKBOOK Write this word in full capital letters, place a mirror above the word and perpendicular to the paper, and what do you get? "CHECKBOOK."

checkmate   You may think that this word originated from the practice of checking your (chess) mate. But in fact the word comes from the Arabic *shāh māt,* meaning "the king is dead." The word *shah* also appears, for example, in *"Shah of Iran."*

checkmating   Remove a few letters from this word and scramble the rest. The appropriate result is "catch king."

chelonian   This sounds as if it might mean "pertaining to cellos." In fact, it means "pertaining to tortoises or turtles."

chiaroscuro   This word means literally "light dark."

Chicago   This place-name is "pregnant" with twins: "chic" and "ago."

chiliad   This word may appear to have something to do with chili, but in fact it denotes a group of one thousand or a period of one thousand years (a millennium).

chimes   Some experts, including Wilfred Funk, have said that this word is among the ten most beautiful words in the English language.

Chi-n-chi-ku-ri-n   Perhaps the longest word in the Japanese language, this is a slang expression for "someone who is very short."

CHOICE   Write this word in full capital letters, place a mirror above the word and perpendicular to the paper, and what do you get? "CHOICE."

Cholmondeley   This British place-name is pronounced "chumley."

Christian   Remove a few letters from this word and scramble the rest. The appropriate result is "saint." And by the way, if you scramble the letters in "saintliness," you'll get "least in sins."

Christianity   This word, when scrambled, contains a sentence that aptly expresses a major tenet of the religion: "I cry that I sin."

Christians   This word does not always mean what it appears to mean. For there is one American city whose residents—even if they are Jews, Muslims, or Zoroastrians—are all referred to as Christians. That city is Corpus Christi (Body of Christ), Texas.

chug   This word comes from the sound of chugging; it's onomatopoeic.

chump   Write this word out in longhand, then turn the paper upside down, and what does it say? "Chump."

Churchtown   This town in Britain is pronounced "chowzen."

Cilohocla   This was the name of a noted racing greyhound of the 1970s. The name is "alcoholic" spelled backward.

cinema   Scramble the letters of "cinema" and you can come up with "iceman" or "anemic."

Cirencester   This British place-name is pronounced "sisseter."

Cisestrian   Could you have guessed that this is the word for a resident of Chichester, England?

cistern   Now, kids, you can both play. First it'll be brother's turn, then cistern!

Citian, Cityite These are legitimate words for *some* people who live in cities. You see, most city dwellers call themselves "city folks" or "urbanites." But the residents of some cities prefer Citian or Cityite. To explain: people in Winston-Salem, North Carolina, call themselves Twin Citians; in Kansas there are Dodge Citians, and of course there are Oklahoma Citians, Jersey Cityites, Bay Citians (in Texas), and Kansas Citians or Kansas Cityans (in Kansas and Missouri). But in case you think you've gotten the hang of this, beware! For people in Vatican City call themselves Vaticanians; in Mexico City, Mexicanos or Chilangos; in Salt Lake City, Salt Lakers; in Panama City, Panamanians; and in Durham City, England, Dunelmains (go figure).

civic This word is a palindrome; it reads the same way backward and forward.

clang This word comes from the sound of clanging; it's onomatopoeic.

classic Why no student came to school?

clatter This word comes from the sound of clattering; it's onomatopoeic.

claustrophobia Fear of Santa Claus?

cleanliness Scramble the letters of this word and the appropriate result is "all niceness."

Cleveland Not only does the name of the city in Ohio have nothing to do with President Grover Cleveland, but in fact it has nothing to do with *anyone* named Cleveland. It was named for General Moses Cleaveland.

clothespins Scramble this word, and you'll see what your clothespins are really thinking: "so let's pinch."

clunk This word comes from the sound of a clunk; it's onomatopoeic.

coach This word comes originally from the Hungarian phrase *kocsi szekér,* "a cart made in Kocs" (a town in Hungary). So when we use the word "coach," we're naming a place, not a thing. The thing is a cart, which, if we were to use the original phrase, would be called a *szekér,* not a coach.

Cockburnspath You might never have guessed that this town in the British Isles is pronounced "coburnspath."

cockup This word should have no nasty connotations. It actually means—can we say this in print?—"a hat or cap turned up in front."

coincide When it gets too rainy it's best to coincide?

collapse He collapse his hands whenever someone says something with which he agrees?

colligate This word may appear to be the name of a gate or a misspelling of a brand of toothpaste or of "collegiate." But it's none of those. It means "to group together according to an underlying principle."

comate This may look like a word that means "cause to fall into a coma." In fact, it means "hairy" or "shaggy." It's related to "comb."

comatose Pedicurists request?

commentator An ordinary potato?

committees Scramble the letters of this word and the appropriate result is "cost me time."

---

compassionateness   Scramble this word, and you'll see what having compassionateness does: "stamps one as so nice."

compensation   Remove a few letters from this word and scramble the rest. The appropriate result is "coins."

COMSUBCOMNEAMCOMHEDSUPPACT   This is the longest acronym in the English language, courtesy of the U.S. Navy. It stands for COMmander, SUBordinate COMmand, Naval forces, Eastern Atlantic and Mediterranean, COMmander HEaDquarters SUPPort ACTivities! The navy does have an odd way of creating acronyms.

conceit   If you look really hard, you just conceit!

condemnation   Scramble this word, and let it speak for it-self: "I connote damn."

confectionery   This is probably the only English word in which you can find the letters that constitute "forty-one" and "forty-nine."

confines   The idea of "friendly confines" didn't exist until baseball's Ernie Banks coined it to refer to the Chicago Cubs when they were playing in Wrigley Field, their hometown ballpark.

CONSCIENCE   This is a fitting acronym for the apparently defunct Committee On National Student Citizenship In Every National Case of Emergencies.

consensus   This word is *not* spelled "conc*e*nsus." Of course, many people would probably find it easier to spell it that way, thinking of a consensus as the taking of a *census* of people's opinions. However, the word is related not to "census" but rather to "consent" (agreement) and is literally a "feeling (as in "sense") together (*con*)."

---

conservative Scramble the letters of this word and the appropriate result is "not vice versa."

considerate Scramble the letters of this word and the appropriate result is "care is noted."

consternation Scramble the letters of this word and the appropriate result is "one cannot stir."

constraint Scramble the letters of this word and the appropriate result is "cannot stir."

container Another word for "container" is inside this word. It's "can."

contaminate If you remove "conmae" from "contaminate," you're liable to "taint" something.

contemplation Scramble the letters of this word and the appropriate result is "on mental topic."

conveniently This is probably the shortest English word in which you can find the letters that constitute "ninety-one."

conventional You can turn "conventional" into "novel" simply by removing a few letters and scrambling those that remain.

conversation Scramble the letters of this word and the appropriate result is "voices rant on."

conversationalist Scramble the letters of this word and the appropriate result is " 'tis one vocal strain."

COOKIE Write this word out all in full capital letters, place a mirror above the word and perpendicular to the paper, and what do you get? "COOKIE."

---

cornflakes There was a time when, strictly speaking, we could not have legitimately written this word as we do now. For the phrase was originally a company's registered trademark, a brand name, and therefore was supposed to be capitalized and in some instances, to carry a trademark symbol: Corn Flakes™.

counterfeit This is one of the few English words, if not the only English word, in which you can find the letters that constitute "fourteen."

countessship Three *s*'s in a row!

country Ultimately this comes from the Vulgar Latin phrase *contra ta regio,* meaning "opposite region." What's left of that phrase is mainly the "opposite"—or *contra/countr*—part, rather than the part that described what a country actually is: a *regio,* or region. Presumably, the *y,* or the *ry,* at the end of "country" is all that remains of the *regio* part of the phrase. The idea behind being an opposite region was that a country is the area that lies before, or opposite, you.

countryside Is the countryside under the city? The question might seem ridiculous. But if you remove a few letters from "countryside" and scramble the rest, you'll discover "under city."

coupon If this word were spelled as it is sometimes pronounced—"q-pon"—it would be the only four-letter word completely in reverse alphabetical order.

cousin This word is a shortened form of the Latin "consobrinus." *Con* means "together," and *sobrinus* comes from *sosrinos,* which means "cousin on mother's side." (*Sosrinos* is from *soror*—"sister.")

---

coward   The only coward I know is "moo"!

crackle   This word comes from the sound of crackling; it's onomatopoeic.

crapulence   This word has nothing to do with . . . well, you know. It pertains to excessive drinking and hangovers.

crash   This word comes from the sound of a crash; it's onomatopoeic.

crayfish   A crayfish ain't a fish; it's a crustacean. The Old French word for it was *crevis,* which to English speakers sounds like "crayfish."

critically   This word can be split into two opposites: "critic" and "ally."

crownwork   Ignore the first and last letters in this word, and see what's left: "rownwor." It's not a real word, but it does read the same way backward and forward. (You knew there had to be some reason for its inclusion in this dictionary.)

crumbled   This word is "pregnant" with twins: "crumb" and "led."

crunch   In an August 1946 poll taken by the National Association of Teachers of Speech, this word was named one of the ten worst-sounding words in the English language.

culprit   This word comes from a sixteenth-century legal abbreviation, "Cul.prit," the abbreviation for *Culpable: prest d'averrer (nostre bille),* meaning "Guilty: ready to aver [our indictment]." The legal abbreviation became our word for a guilty person.

CURB   This is the fitting acronym for the Campaign on the Use and Restriction of Barbiturates.

curtail   Another word for "curtail" is inside this word. It's "cut."

curtailment   Scramble the letters of this word and you get "terminal cut."

custody   I like anything that tastes like custard—the more custody, the better!

customers   Remove a few letters from this word and you get where customers go: "stores."

Cwmtwrch   This vowelless creature is actually a Welsh place-name.

D

Dabney   This name is actually a shortened version of the French name d'Aubigny, which means "from Aubigny." It seems that the English were quick to adopt, and adapt, the language of the French-speaking Normans who conquered Britain in 1066. The apostrophe was dropped, and few people now realize that the remaining *d* represented "from."

dairyman   Ignore the last letter of this word, read the remainder in reverse, and what do you get? "A myriad."

Dalziel   This British place-name is pronounced "dee-ell."

dame   In 1933 a Hollywood studio banned this word from its films because the word was considered "unsuitable."

Dangerfield   The comedian who gets no respect takes his surname from "de Angerville," meaning "from or of Angerville." Angerville is a place in Normandy—really, it is!

Darlene   Amazingly, this name can be scrambled into four other first names: Darleen, Leander, Leandre, and Learned.

Datsun   Manufactured in 1933, the original Datsun, the forerunner of Nissan Motor Company's automobiles, was called DAT, from the initials of the three financial backers of the Japanese Kwaishimsha Motor Car Works: K. *D*en, R. *A*oyama, and A. *T*akeuchi. In the early years the name was changed to Datson, to signify "son of DAT." Later, because "son" sounded like the Japanese word for "loss," the name became "Datsun."

Daughtery, Daltry   These surnames come from "de Hauterive," one who is from Hauterive in Orne, Normandy.

dawn   Some experts, such as Wilfred Funk, have said that this is among the ten most beautiful words in the English language.

debate   De fisherman catches de fish by using debate?

debonair   This is actually a three-word fusion. It comes from the French *"de bon air,"* literally "of *(de)* good *(bon)* origin or character *(air)*." Remember that in English the word "air" can also mean "manner" or "quality."

debt   For those who complain about English spellings not making sense, let us try to explain the logic of one odd spelling. The word "debt" was borrowed from the French *dette*. So why, you ask, put a *b* in it? Well, it seems that the language reformers of the sixteenth century decided that "debt" better reflected the Latin word *debitum,* which was the origin of the French *dette*. So in a sense, they put the *b* back, even though they continued to pronounce the word without the *b* sound. Go figure!

decimal point   Remove a few letters from this phrase and scramble the rest. The appropriate result is "I'm a dot."

---

declaration   Scramble the letters of this word and the appropriate result is "an oral edict."

decollate   This word may appear to be the spelling of "decorate" by someone who has difficulty pronouncing *r*. In fact, the word means "to behead." The word "collar," also related to the neck and head, has the same root.

decorated   Three other words are hidden in this word. Take the first letter and then every third letter, and you'll get "dot." Now find another word by taking every third letter, starting with the *e*: "ere." Finally, find still another word by taking every third letter, starting with the *c*: "cad."

decussate   This word looks as if it might mean "tending to cuss or use profanity." Actually, it means "to intersect" and is obliquely related to the Roman numeral for ten (X).

Deewhy   The answer to the question "Dee why?" is simple. Deewhy is the name of a lagoon in New South Wales. Remarkably, the lagoon is shaped like a *D* and a *Y*!

defenselessness   This is one of the longest words using only the letter *e* for its vowel.

deficiencies   This word breaks the spelling rule, "*i* before *e*, except when preceded by a *c*"—and breaks it twice.

degenerescence   This word, along with "indivisibility," is perhaps the longest word in the English language having only one vowel, which is repeated six times! Degenerescence is the tendency to degenerate, or the process of degenerating.

deified   This word is a palindrome; it reads the same way backward and forward.

deltiology This may appear to be the word for a study of the Mississippi delta. In fact, it refers to the hobby of postcard collecting. The word originates from the Greek *deltion,* meaning "small writing tablet."

demisemi This strange-looking prefix—strange-looking, that is, to anyone who is not familiar with music—means "one-quarter" in music. It is literally a hybrid comprising words from two different languages: the French word for "one-half," *demi,* and the Latin word for "one-half," *semi.* A half of a half is a quarter.

demotic This word may appear to mean "demonic lunatic." In fact, it means "common" or "popular," especially in reference to language. "Democracy" contains the same root.

dendriform This word might appear to mean "in the shape of dandruff." In fact, it means "resembling a tree." The word "tree" is itself ultimately related to the Greek root (pardon the pun) "dendro."

denial In de country of Egypt is de river we call denial.

denier Read this word backward and you get "reined." Some wordsmiths call such a word a semordnilap, a word that forms a different word when read backward.

departed Remove a few letters from this word, and the appropriate result is "dead."

deperm This may appear to be the word for what the hairdresser does when removing one's perm. It actually means "to demagnetize partly a ship's steel hull to protect the ship from magnetic mines." "Perm" in this case is short for "permanent magnetism."

depreciations   Scramble the letters of this word and the appropriate result is "no praise cited."

derange   Mix up a deranged person with a grandiose personality and they may become angered, indeed enraged. They might even pick up a grenade. By the way, scrambling the letters of "derange" generates "grandee," "angered," "enraged," and "grenade."

deride   Step out of the car? (Well, if we can "deplane," why can't we "deride"?)

derision   Scramble the letters of "ironside" and you have "derision."

dermatoglyphics   This is one of the longest English words that has no repeated letters. The word means "the science of fingerprints."

designation   Remove a few letters from this word and scramble the rest. The appropriate result is "denoting."

despair   You'd better get despair tire out of de trunk!

desperation   Scramble the letters of this word and the appropriate result is "a rope ends it."

destiny   Scramble the letters of this word and this is the appropriate result: "It's y' end."

detartrated   This is a word that word lovers wish existed. Amazingly, it reads the same way backward and forward. Unfortunately it's not in any legitimate dictionaries. (Is *this* a legitimate dictionary? Hmm.) By the way, if it were a genuine word, it would mean, roughly, "separated from tartaric acid."

devil Believe it or not, there is absolutely no "evil" in the "devil"—at least, etymologically speaking. The word "devil" comes not from "evil" but from the Greek *diabolos,* as in "diabolical." *Dia* means "across" or "through," and *bolos* means "throw," as in "ballistic." The idea was that the devil throws across you or is, in other words, deceptive. You might say that the devil throws a curveball. (Incidentally, "devil" spelled backwards is "lived.")

dialogue This is one of the shortest English words in which all the vowels appear—and appear only once.

DICEBOX Write this word out all in capitalized letters, place a mirror above the word and perpendicular to the paper, and what do you get? "DICEBOX."

dictum Be original. Don't do what every dictum and Harry has already done!

dieresis This may appear to be the name of a form of diarrhea. In fact, it is the name of a two-dot pronunciation symbol, as in "naïve."

dilate I'd rather dilate than die too early!

dinner This word has been shortened to death. For "dinner" is a dramatic shortening of a word whose heart—or at least it's jejunum—has been torn from it. The original word was much closer to "disjejuner," which in turn came from the Latin *disjejunare,* meaning, literally, "away fast," in other words, "breakfast." (Dinner is, after all, a kind of breaking of the fast, too.) "Dis" means "away" (or "break"), and "jejunare" means "fast." The jejunum is the second part of the intestine, which is thought of as being empty when one has not eaten for a long time. Hope you haven't lost your appetite for dinner—disjejuner, that is.

diploma   When de water is coming out de wrong end of de pipe, it's time to call diploma?

diplomacy   Scramble the letters of this word and you get what some people think of diplomacy: "mad policy."

diplomatic   Remove a few letters from this word and scramble the rest. The appropriate result is "politic."

directorship   Prince Charles never wrecked his ship. But Princess directorship! Clarification for persons reading this book in the twenty-first century: After the passing of Queen Elizabeth II, her eldest son, Prince Charles, became the last king of England. Before taking the throne, and before he married Madonna, he was married briefly to Princess Di. (Well, some of it's true!)

discrimination   This word is "pregnant" with quintuplets: "disc," "rim," "in," "at," and "ion."

Dishmaugh   This odd name of a U.S. city was once known as "du Chemin," a French term for a roadway. To the later, non-French settlers, "du Chemin" sounded like "Dishmaugh."

Disney   The surname of the master of animated entertainment is actually a shortening of the French "d'Isigny," which meant "from Isigny." The English were quick to adopt—and adapt—the language of the French-speaking Normans who conquered Britain in 1066. The apostrophe was dropped, and few people now realize that the remaining *d* represented "from."

dissimulate   Remove a few letters from this word and scramble the rest. The appropriate result is "mislead."

divorce Remove a few letters from this word and scramble the rest. The appropriate result is "over."

Dmitri Read the first part of this name backward (imd); then read the rest backward (irt). The result: "I'm dirt"!

Dnieper This name of a river in Europe actually comes from Sarmatic *don,* which means "river" (related to the *dan* in "Danube") and *ipr,* which means "river." Thus, "Dnieper" means "River River," and if you call it the Dnieper River, then it's the River River River!

Doe There are really Doe families and, yes, even real people named John Doe. One of the origins of the name is the French *de Eu,* one who is "from Eu," an area of Seine-Maritime.

dogma Married to dog's paw?

Donora This city in Pennsylvania takes its name from William H. *Don*ner, the president of an improvement company, and *Nora* Mellon, the wife of a stockholder.

Doolittle Who are people with that surname fooling? They're not fooling anyone with that extra *o.* For the name means just what it sounds like it means: "do little" or, in other words, "the lazy one."

Dora Read this feminine name backward and you get a male name, specifically "a Rod."

doraphobia This may appear to mean a fear of persons named Dorothy. In fact, it is an abnormal fear of touching the skin or the fur of an animal.

dormitory Scramble the letters of this word and the appropriate result is "dirty room."

Dozier This surname comes from *de Osier,* an Old French term referring to someone who lives near a willow tree or grove.

drawing Contrary to what you might think, no drawing has ever been done in a drawing room—etymologically speaking, that is. Originally, this room was called the "withdrawing room." Quite simply, it was the place to which the womenfolk would withdraw while the menfolk talked about politics and such.

drit No, this is not a misspelling of "dirt." It is, rather, a very old spelling of "dirt," for by the year 1300, filth was described as "drit." Yet by the linguistic process known as metathesis, the *r* and *i* sounds gradually were inverted, and soon "drit" became "dirt." Somehow "dirt" just doesn't sound as dirty as "drit," does it?

dromedarian Scramble the letters of this word and the appropriate result is "a nomad rider."

dromedary As you may recall, a dromedary is a one-humped camel. Yet the word itself ultimately does not mean either "camel"—or "one-humped" but simply "running." In fact, it is only one-half of an ancient Greek name for the animal, *dromas kamelas,* meaning "running camel." Now, wouldn't it be easier to remember that a dromedary is a kind of camel if it were called a "dromedary camelas"? Or perhaps a "running camel"? Well, maybe not. Why not just a "one-hump"?

dry ice There was a time when, strictly speaking, we could not have legitimately written this phrase in this way. The phrase was originally a company's registered trademark, or brand name, and therefore required a capital letter and, in some uses, a trademark symbol: Dry Ice™.

duchessship Three *s*'s in a row!

duoliteral This word has all the vowels, each appearing only once and in reverse alphabetical order. It means "consisting of two letters."

dupe This word probably comes from the Middle French phrase *de huppe,* meaning "of the hoopoe." The hoopoe is a bird that is considered stupid-looking and presumably easily deceived. So the next time you get taken, say "I've been de-hupped!"

dynamite Scramble the letters of this word and the appropriate result will be "I may dent."

E

each   Before your very eyes, this word will become another word if you simply move the first letter to the end. Move the *e* to the end, and you get "ache." Notice also that the word now has a completely different sound.

earthquakes   Remove a few letters from this word and scramble the rest. The appropriate result is "shake."

eaves   This word looks like a plural, but it's not. The plural of "eaves" is "eaveses." "Eaves" is from the Old English *euese* and the Icelandic *ups,* meaning "a projection"—in other words, something that goes *over.*

Ebro   This name of this river in northern Spain comes from the Celtic *iber,* which means "river." Thus the Ebro River is the River River.

echoic   Before your very eyes, this word will become another word if you simply move the first letter to the end. Move the *e* to the end, and you get "choice." Notice also that the word now has a completely different sound.

eclipse   The barber: he shaves, he cuts, he snips, eclipse?

economy   Perhaps this word should be spelled "oiconomy." It comes from the Greek *oikonomia*. Oink, oink! And by the way, an oikologist is a homemaker!

edifice   Perhaps this word should be spelled "aedifice." It comes from the Latin *aedificium*. After all, we don't spell "aerial" as "erial."

Edward Gorey   What would you do if you were a writer named Edward Gorey and you wanted to come up with fifteen different pseudonyms? Here's what Gorey came up with: Dogear Wryde, Wardore Edgy, Dreary Wodge, Drew Dogyear, Regera Dowdy, G. E. Deadworry, D. Awdrey-Gore, Roger Addyew, Grey Redwoad, Dedge Yarrow, Orde Graydew, Waredo Dyrge, Deary Rewdgo, Dewda Yorger, and Addee Gorrwy. In so naming himself, Edward Gorey has the distinction of perhaps having more pseudonyms that are scramblings of the letter of his real name than any other writer. So why not "E. Edgar Wordy"?

eeeeve   Have you ever seen a word with four *e*'s in a row? Well, now you have! The word is the local name for a Hawaiian bird, the iiwi.

efficiencies   This word breaks the spelling rule, "*i* before *e*, except when preceded by a *c*"—and breaks it twice.

egg   The "egg" in the phrase, "egg on," has nothing to do with eggs. Rather, it comes from the Old Norse *eggja* (to urge), related to "edge." The idea is that if you are being egged on, you are edged toward taking action.

egocentric   You can transpose the first and second letters of this word and come up with another word, "geocentric."

Eighty Eight   This is the name not only of a number but also of a city in Kentucky. It seems that the town is 8.8 miles from Glasgow, the county seat of Barren County. The postmaster apparently felt that it would be easier just to write "88." And so that's the name the townspeople took.

elapse   The dog licks people and elapse water?

elliptical   Another word for a kiss?

emanate   Before your very eyes, this word will become another word if you simply move the first letter to the end. Move the *e* to the end, and—ta-dah—you have "manatee." Remarkable, truly remarkable.

Emb   Wouldn't this be a great name for a city in Arkansas? Emb, Ark.—embark!

Embarrass   This is the name of a city in Wisconsin, but its origin has nothing to do with embarrassment. The name is a misspelling—actually an Americanization—of the French *embarrassée*. The French-Canadian lumberjacks in the area referred to one of the rivers as Rivière Embarrassée, meaning "tangled river," in reference to the fact that logs often got jammed in the river.

EMPHASIS   This is an acronym for Evaluation Management using Past History Analysis for Scientific Inventory Simulation.

encore   *"Hinc ad horam! Hinc ad horam!"* After people said that thousands of times over the years, it became simply "encore." *"Hinc ad horam"* was a Vulgar Latin phrase meaning "hence" or "from then [*hinc*] to [*ad*] this hour [*horam*]." *Hinc ad horam! Hinc ad horam!*

47

encourage   Another word for "encourage" is inside this word. It's "urge."

endearing   An earring that goes on the end of your ear?

endearment   Scramble the letters of this word and the appropriate result is "tender name."

English   Would you believe that this is the name of an actual city in Indiana? Actually, the city is named for William Hayden English, a late-nineteenth-century vice presidential candidate.

enormity   Scrambled inside of "enormity" is something much "more tiny."

enough   Scramble the letters of this word and you get "one hug."

enrober   Read this word backward and you get "reborne." Some wordsmiths call such a word a semordnilap, a word that forms a different word when read in reverse.

entity   *N, o, p, q, r, s,* and *t?*

entrail   The animal that leaves its entrails might be well advised to shuffle off to the nearest latrine. And how does the animal perform such a feat? Simple: just shuffle the letters in "entrail," and the result will be "latrine." (Of course, other results could be "ratline" and "reliant.")

envy   This word was much more colorful and expressive in its original form. The word was originally "invidia," meaning "to look upon": *in* (upon), *vidia* (to look, as in "video"). After all, we do look very strongly upon the accomplishments or possessions of those of whom we are envious, or en*vid*ious.

epaulet This word for the ornament on the shoulder of a uniform is actually from the Latin word for a flat piece of wood that resembled a shoulder blade: *spatula.* After all, a spatula, which we use to scoop up fried eggs, is somewhat like a blade. (You didn't realize you were using someone's shoulder blade, did you?) So now you know: the ornaments on the shoulder of a uniform are simply another shoulder blade or, if you prefer, a spatula.

epinasty This word may appear to mean "something nasty." In fact, it denotes the movement by which a plant is bent outward and often downward, as when a flower petal unfolds.

epistaxis This word may appear to have something to do with taxis. In fact, it is another word for "nosebleed."

epure This may appear to be the word for a degree of purity. In fact, an epure is a complete architectural drawing, usually traced on a wall or a floor.

equal Perhaps this word should be spelled "aequal," for it comes from the Latin *aequalis.* After all, we don't spell "aerobic" as "erobic."

equation This is one of the shortest English words in which all the vowels appear only once.

escalator There was a time when, strictly speaking, we could not have legitimately written this word in this way. The word was originally a company's registered trademark, or brand name, and therefore required a capital letter and, in some uses, a trademark symbol: Escalator™. The word comes from *"escalating elevator,"* which was patented in 1900 by the Otis Elevator Company for passengers of the Manhattan Elevated Railway. The word is now generic, having been legally adjudged in 1940 to have become public property through popular use.

escalator If she won't give you an answer now, you can always escalator.

esculent This word may appear to pertain to an esculator. In fact, it means "edible."

esquamate This may appear to be what the husband of a squaw is called. In fact, it means "having no scales."

Esso The old Esso Petroleum Company (now the Exxon Corporation) got its name from S.O., the initials of the Standard Oil Company of New Jersey, the chief company of the oil trust set up by John D. Rockfeller.

esteem, estimate Perhaps these words should be spelled "aesteem" and "aestimate," for they both come from the Latin *aestimare,* meaning "to value."

ester Before your very eyes, this word for a type of organic compound will become several other words if you simply keep moving the first letter to the end. Move the *e* to the end, and you get "stere," a unit of measure. Now, again, move the first letter of this new word to the end, and you get "teres," the sixteenth-century spelling of "tears." And again, move the first letter of this new word to the end, and you get "erest," the fourteenth-century spelling of "erst." Once again, move the first letter of this new word to the end, and you get "reste," the sixteenth-century spelling of "rest." And finally, move the first letter of this new word to the end, and you get "ester." Sounds familiar, doesn't it?

Estevan This name of a city in Saskatchewan, Canada, was created from George *Ste*phan and Sir William *Van* Horner, two Canadian Pacific Railroad associates.

etaoin shrdlu   This is an actual English term found in legitimate dictionaries. Most veteran newspaper people will recognize it as the combination of letters produced as a marking slug by a Linotype but not intended to appear in the final printing. It has come to refer to any line of jumbled type or other unintended material appearing in a newspaper. The letters themselves are the twelve most frequently used letters in English. But, no, there is no single word that includes all of them. The following words have been suggested, but you won't see them in any dictionary except this one: "outlanderish" and "tailhounders."

eternal   Why don't we spell this word "eviternal" or "everternal"? Those spellings would more nearly reflect the Latin root of "eternal": *aeviternus,* meaning "of great age." The *aev,* or *ev,* which has disappeared from "eternal," is directly related to the "ev" in "ever" and "medieval." Oh, well, nothing lasts fore'er.

eunoia   This may be the shortest English word having one of each vowel and only one consonant. The word means "alertness of mind and will."

Euodia   This name of a Christian woman mentioned in the New Testament contains one of each vowel and only one consonant.

euouae   This musical term contains six letters, all vowels, and no consonants—an English-language record!

evangelists   They purport to be the agents of God, but some so-called evangelists may really be "evil's agents"! Scramble the word and see.

Evansdale   This name of a city in Iowa holds the distinction of being one of the few place-names—perhaps the only place-name—in the world that ends in "dale" but does not originate from a nearby valley. ("Dale" means "valley." Yes, it's true, Valleydale means "valley valley.") The city also has nothing to do with Dale Evans . . . but you're getting warm. Actually, the city gets its name from William T. *Evans* and *Dale* van Eman, whoever they were.

everlasting   Remove a few letters from this word and scramble the rest. The appropriate result is "eternal."

Ex   Wouldn't this be a great name for a city in Connecticut? Ex, Conn.—ex-con!

exanthem   This word might appear to refer to the national anthem of one's former homeland. In fact, it is the name of an eruptive disease or its symptomatic eruption, as in measles or smallpox, often associated with fever.

Exonian   Could you have guessed that this would be the word for a resident of Exeter, England?

expectant   What to do when you leave crumbs on the floor?

explain   A more "sophisticated" use of this word: "Please don't scramble them; I like my explain."

F

Faaa And you thought the AAA had a monopoly on the three *a*'s! This is the name of a settlement on the west coast of Tahiti.

facetiously This word has all the vowels, including *y*, each appearing only once, in alphabetical order.

fadmongering This word contains two six-letter words, one in the middle, and one on the outside: "monger" and "fading" ("fad" and "ing").

Fairborn This name of a city in Ohio was created by combining parts of the names of two neighboring villages: *Fair*field and Os*born*.

falsehood A phony gangster?

falsities You can remove a lot from falsities, and you still won't change things. For example, remove the "fa" and the "sit" from "falsities," and you'll still have "lies"!

---

families Scramble this word, and you'll discover that families are "life's aim."

FAMOUS This is not just a word but also an acronym. It stands for the French-American Mid-Ocean Undersea Study (of the Mid-Atlantic Ridge).

farcical A very long icicle?

fatal This word is "pregnant" with twins: "fat" and "Al."

featherweight Remove a few letters from this word and scramble the rest. The appropriate result is "a wee fighter."

Feeass Wouldn't this be a great name for a city in Colorado? Feeass, CO—fiasco!

feedback Except for the *k* this eight-letter word contains only the first six letters of the alphabet.

fell The "fell" in the phrase "one fell swoop" has nothing to do with "fall," as in falling upon something. Rather, it once meant "*evil*" and is related to "*fel*on."

female There's no "male" in this word—that is, "female" is not related to "male." Rather, it is a respelling of *femelle*, "a small woman." (Most likely, some males did the respelling.) The "fem" part comes from the Latin *femina*, meaning "woman" (as in "feminine"); the *elle* ending denotes smallness. Perhaps, then, if a woman wants to be thought of as neither small nor a part of the male, she could be called simply a "fem" or a "femina."

feracious This is not a misspelling of "ferocious." In fact, it means "fruitful" or "productive." The "fer" (to bear) root also appears in "conifer," a cone-bearing tree or shrub.

54

Fiat   This name of the car and its manufacturer stems, not from the word "fiat" (decree or authorization), but from the abbreviation of the Italian firm founded in 1899: Fabbrica Italiana Automobili Torino (Turin Automobile Works).

fictionproof   This is one of the longest words beginning and ending with *f.*

fife   This word comes from the sound of a fife; it's onomatopoeic.

Fiji   Notice anything unusual about this word? It contains three consecutive dotted letters, a rarity!

finnif   This word is a palindrome; it reads the same way backward and forward. The word is slang for a five-dollar bill or a five-pound note.

Fishkill   Believe it or not, this small town in New York State has nothing to do with dead fish. It comes from the Dutch *vis kill,* meaning "a stream full of fish." By the way, what does Fishkill Creek, another New York place-name, mean? "A stream full of fish creek"!

flammable   This word looks as if it should mean the opposite of "inflammable," but of course it means the same.

flatulent   In an August 1946 poll taken by the National Association of Teachers of Speech, this word was recognized as one of the ten worst-sounding words in the English language. By the way, the best-sounding definition of "flatulent" is "affected with gas in the stomach or intestines." We can't say what the worst-sounding definition is.

flavescent   This word may appear to describe some element of flavor. In fact, it means "turning yellow."

---

fleer This word may appear to mean "one who flees," but it doesn't always mean that. Sometimes it means "to laugh, grin, or grimace in a coarse way, or to sneer." It is related to the Norwegian *flire,* meaning "to giggle."

float Scramble the letters of this word and the appropriate result is "aloft."

Florala This is the name of a city on the Florida-Alabama state line. Wonder how they came up with the name.

fluster The opposite condition of being flustered is embedded in this word. Just scramble it and you'll get "restful."

fool's paradise Remove a few letters from this phrase and scramble the rest. The appropriate result is "false road."

footle This word may appear to mean "a little foot." In fact, it means "to waste time" or "to talk or act foolishly."

footstool Ignore the first and last letters in this word, and see what's left: "ootstoo." It's not a real word, but it does read the same way backward or forward. (You knew there had to be some reason for its presence in this dictionary.)

forbidding The attitude of an auctioneer?

forester Scramble the letters of this word and you get what the forester is: "for trees."

Formica Although the name of this plastic laminate and its manufacturer appears to be related to the Latin root for "ant" *(formic),* it actually has nothing whatever to do with ants. Rather, it is the name of a natural resin substitute for mica, created in 1913 by two young American scientists, Herb Faber and Dan O'Connor, who were seeking an insulation material for electrical wiring. The Formica Corporation later became part of American Cyanamid.

fortnight   This word is actually missing a few vowels. The word was originally "fourteen-night." Wouldn't it be a lot easier to remember that a fortnight is two weeks if we simply called it what it is?

fortunate   Scramble the letters of this word and the appropriate result is "turn o' fate."

fragile   "Fragile" is indeed a fragile word. If you remove the *g* and *e,* it's still "frail."

FREDERICK   This is the acronymic name of the Family Robot for Entertainment Discussion and Education, Retrieval of Information, and Collation of Knowledge.

fretum   This word may appear to refer to something one frets over. In fact, it means "an arm of the sea" or "a strait."

friable   This may appear to mean "capable of being fried." In fact, it means "easily crushed or pulverized."

frontiersman   Remove a few letters from "frontiersman" and scramble the rest. You'll discover where the frontiersman is usually headed: "to far rim."

fungible   This may appear to refer to having fungi. In fact, it means "interchangeable, as economic goods."

funic   This may appear to mean "related to fun." In fact, it means "pertaining to the umbilical cord."

fyyryryn   This four *y* word is a Middle English spelling of "fire iron."

G

gag This word comes from the sound of someone gagging; it's onomatopoeic.

Gam Wouldn't this be a great name for a city in Utah? Gam, UT—gamut!

Gamaliel This middle name of President Warren Harding is, when read backward, two female names: Leila and Mag.

gangavatarana This is one of the longest words using only the letter *a* for its vowel. The word refers to the descent of the Ganges River, which, in Hindu mythology, fell on the head of the god Siva.

gangrene This word is not spelled "gan*green*." For even though, when gangrene sets in, the affected part might turn green, the word has nothing to do with the color green. The word comes ultimately from the Greek *gangraina*, meaning "gnawing sore." The Greek word for "gnaw" was *gran,* and it is speculated that the word "gangraina" may have originated from a simple duplication of *gran* (*gran-gran*) in order to suggest the intensity of the gnawing pain. Hence, perhaps "gangrene" should really be "gnawgnaw."

gateman Read this word backward and you get "nametag." Some wordsmiths call such a word a semordnilap, a word that forms a different word when read in reverse.

gelatin Before your very eyes, this word will become another word if you simply move the first letter to the end. Move the *g* to the end, and you get "elating."

genteel This word is "pregnant" with twins: "gent" and "eel."

gentleman Remove a few letters from this word and scramble the rest. The appropriate result is "elegant."

geometry Geometry! I've got limbs. I've got leaves. I've got bark. Yes, indeed, I'm a tree!

Georgia This is the name of both a southern U.S. state and a southern Russian republic. In reality, the Russian Georgia is entirely unrelated in origin to the American Georgia. The American Georgia, of course, comes from the proper name, George. The Russian Georgia is called Georgia only because the original Russian name for that region—Gruzia—sounded, to English ears, like "Georgia." The name Gruzia comes from the name of the region's inhabitants, Gurz, or Gurdzh.

georgic This word may appear to be related to someone named George. In fact, it means "pertaining to agriculture and rural affairs" or "rustic." After all, the name George itself comes from a word meaning "farmer"; the "geo" root relates to the earth.

Gernigeria The name of Nigeria might be so spelled to resemble more nearly its original meaning. For Nigeria takes its name from its chief river, the Niger, which in turn comes from the native name for the river: *gher n-gherea,* meaning "river among rivers." Thus, in a sense "Nigeria" means "among rivers." Only when another "ger" is added to the beginning of the word does it more nearly reflect its origin: Gernigeria. (Note that "Nigeria" is not related to the Latin *niger,* meaning "black.")

Gibraltar   This port was not named for someone named Gibraltar. It was named for Tarik, a Saracen conqueror. "Gibraltar" is actually a corruption of Jebel el Tarik, which means "the mountain of Tarik."

giggle   This word is noteworthy because it's a fairly long computer word—that is, when it's written in block-style, all capitalized, and turned upside down, it forms computer-style numbers. "GIGGLE" turned upside down becomes 376616!

gingerbread   This word looks as if it's related to "bread." Yet gingerbread is not, and has never been, bread. Cake, yes; bread, no. In fact, the original word for "ginger" was "gimgibre." Ultimately, the "bre" part of the word became "bread." Why? Because that's what it looks like. And cake isn't all that far from being bread, is it?

Glaswegian   Could you have guessed that this would be the word for a resident of Glasgow, Scotland?

Glenelg   This word is a palindrome; it reads the same way backward and forward. Glenelg is the name of a resort near Adelaide, Australia.

globes   This word is noteworthy because it's a fairly long computer word—that is, when it's written in block-style capitals and turned upside down, it forms computer-style numbers. "GLOBES" turned upside down becomes 538079!

Gobi   Shouldn't the Gobi Desert really be simply Kobi, for the name comes from the Mongolian word for "desert": *kobi.* Saying "Gobi Desert" is like saying "desert desert."

godessship   Three *s*'s in a row!

Godmanchester   You might never guess that the name of this town in the British Isles is pronounced "gumsister" or "gonshister."

golden   Some experts, including Wilfred Funk, have said that this is one of the ten most beautiful words in the English language.

gonorrhea   Some experts, including Willard Espy, have said that this is one of the ten most beautiful—beautiful-sounding, that is—words in the English language.

gossamer   Some experts, including Willard Espy, have said that this is one of the ten most beautiful words in the English language.

GOSSIP   This word is also the appropriate acronym for the Generalized Organizational System Summarizer and Information Processor. It makes gossiping sound respectable, doesn't it? The next time someone tells you that you're a gossip, just tell them what it stands for!

Gramercy   This name of a park in Manhattan comes from *krume marisje,* a Dutch term meaning "crooked little marsh." To the later non-Dutch New Yorkers, though *krume marisje* sounded like "Gramercy."

grandfather   Did you know that "grandfather" literally has mixed parentage? "Grand" is from the French, and "father" is English.

---

grave Even though being put into a grave may be a grave (serious) situation, there's no adjective "grave" in the noun "grave"—that is, the origin of the adjective meaning "serious" is not related to the noun meaning "tomb." The adjective comes from the Latin *gravis,* meaning "heavy," as in "*grav*-ity." Indeed, we speak of the gravity, or seriousness, of a situation. Also, those who have a heavy burden of sorrow *grieve,* that word coming from the same Latin source. Yet the noun comes from the Old English *grafan,* meaning "to dig," from which we also get "groove" and "en*grave*."

great-great-great-great-great-great-grand-niece-in-law This is one of perhaps only three words in the English language having nine hyphens!

Greek "That's Greek to me." Well, maybe it is, but, in fact, in Spain and Russia the expression is "That's Chinese to me." And in Germany people say, "That's Spanish to me." The Polish say, "I'm listening to a Turkish sermon." Honest—we're not making this stuff up, you know.

Greensburgher Could you have guessed that this is the word for a resident of Greensboro, North Carolina? Why not "Greensboroer" or "Greensboroian"? Well, on second thought . . .

grope In an August 1946 poll taken by the National Association of Teachers of Speech, this word was recognized as one of the ten worst-sounding words in the English language.

Guam This place-name could really be San Juan. The island was first sighted on Saint John's Day in 1521 by Spanish explorers under Magellan. "Saint John" in Spanish is "San Juan." But this San Juan, unlike the one in Puerto Rico, was corrupted into "Guam."

Guamanian Could you have guessed that a Guamanian is a resident of Guam? The residents apparently thought that it sounded better than "Guamian."

gulp This word comes from the sound of a gulp; it's onomatopoeic.

gust One of the obscure meanings of this word is actually "inclination" or "liking." Believe it or not, it's the antonym of "disgust"—get it?

guts In 1933 a Hollywood studio banned this word from all its films because the word was considered unsuitable!

gymnopaedic This word contains four consecutive letters in alphabetical order. It means "hatched naked."

gypsyphy This is one of the longest words using only the letter *y* for its vowel.

H

H. A. Largelamb This pseudonym was once used by Alexander Graham Bell. It's "A. Graham Bell" scrambled.

Haecstaréttarmálaflutningsmaôur This is perhaps the longest word in the Icelandic language! It means "a barrister of the Supreme Court."

Hagenaar Could you have guessed that this would be the word for a resident of The Hague, in the Netherlands?

hah This word comes from the sound of a laugh; it's ono-matopoeic. The word first appeared around the year 1000.

halibut Is halibut halibut? Or is it only halibut at special times and simply but at other times? The answer to the first question is "Yes and no. It's halibut, but it's also but." The an-swer to the second question is "Maybe." On the remote chance that those answers have not clarified the issue, let us explain. The word "halibut," the name of a flatfish, means lit-erally "holy butte"—holy because it was eaten especially on holy days, and "butte" because that is—or was—the name of the flatfish. So is it "halibut," "butte," or just plain "but"? You must decide. (A sign outside a Holiday Inn: TRY OUR SEAFOOD PLATTER—FOR THE HALIBUT.)

hallah This word is a palindrome; it reads the same way backward and forward. Hallah (or challah) is a kind of bread eaten especially by Jews on the Sabbath.

Hamamelidaceae This is the longest word composed entirely of letters from the first half of the alphabet, *a* to *m*. It is the name of a family of shrubs and trees including witch hazel and related plants.

hamiform This word may appear to mean "ham-shaped." In fact, it means "hook-shaped."

handicap Everyday headwear?

hangar Nothing hangs in a hangar. The word is actually closer to "anger" than "hanger," for it originates from the French *angars,* meaning "shed," and is unrelated to "hang."

Hannah This name is a palindrome; it reads the same way backward and forward.

Hantsian Could you have guessed that a Hantsian is a resident of Hampshire, England?

Haligonian Could you have guessed that this is the word for a resident of Halifax, Nova Scotia?

Happisburgh This British place-name is pronounced "hayzburra."

hardship Icebreaker!

harvesting Remove a few letters from this word and scramble the rest. The appropriate result is "grains."

headmistress   A woman to whom a married man goes when he desires an intellectual conversation?

headmistressship   Three *s*'s in a row.

headstone   Scramble the letters of this word and you get "one's death."

hearthstone   Scramble the letters of this word and the appropriate result is "heat's throne."

hedonism   A belief that the other guy did it?

helicopter   Remove a few letters from this word and scramble the rest. The appropriate result is "pilot."

Hell   Did you know that Hell is in Michigan? Yes, indeed, Hell is an actual town in Michigan. (And you thought it was Detroit!)

Hemaruka   This city in Saskatchewan gets its name from someone's four daughters: *He*len, *Ma*rgaret, *Ru*th, and *Kat*hleen. Honest!

hereafter   This word has a phantom antonym—a phantonym: "therefore," which isn't really the antonym of "hereafter" but looks as if it could be.

hesitater   Scramble the letters of "hesitater" and you have "heartiest." Scramble them again and you have "earthiest."

hétérogénéité   This French word may well hold the record for the greatest number of accents.

heterosexuality   This is probably the shortest English word in which you can find the letters that constitute "sixty-three."

hibernates What's in "hibernates"? Just scramble the letters and you'll discover that "the bear's in."

Hibernianism Remove a few letters from this word and scramble the rest. The appropriate result is "Irishman."

hiccup This word comes from the sound of a hiccup; it's onomatopoeic.

high-fed This hyphenated seven-letter word contains each (and only each) letter in the alphabet from *d* to *i*.

hijinks Notice anything unusual about this word? It contains three consecutive dotted letters—a rarity!

hiss This word comes from the sound of hissing; it's onomatopoeic.

hominid This word may appear to mean "pertaining to hominy grits." In fact, it means "a creature resembling a human being."

homogeneity This is probably the shortest English word in which you can find the letters that constitute "eighty-one."

homosexual This word is a hybrid, a word with multiple origins—that is, *homo* is of Greek origin, and *sexual* is from the Latin.

honey Write this word out in longhand, turn the paper upside down, and what does it say? It's still "honey"!

honk This word comes from the sound made by a horn; it's onomatopoeic.

hoodlum This word may actually have come about as a result of a printer's error. The printer mistook "noodlum" for "hoodlum." And where, you might ask, did the word "nood-lum" come from? Some maintain that "Noodlum" is back-slang: a reverse spelling of Muldoon, the name of the long-ago leader of a San Francisco gang.

HOOKED   Print this word in full capital letters, place a mirror above the word and perpendicular to the paper, and what do you get? "HOOKED."

hope   The "hope" in the phrase, "forlorn hope," has nothing to do with the word we know as "hope"! Rather, the phrase comes from the Dutch *verloren hoop,* literally "lost troop"— the first soldiers to go into battle, who have little chance of re-turning alive.

Horse Linto   This odd California place-name actually has nothing to do with any horse. The name comes from the Indian village name, Haslintah, which sounded like "Horse Linto."

hospitable   Operating room table?

hospital   Remove a few letters from this word and scramble the rest. The appropriate result is "ail spot."

housebroken   In 1933 a Hollywood studio banned this word from its films because it was considered unsuitable.

howl   This word gets its name from the sound of a howl; it's onomatopoeic.

Hughmilleria   This is part of the formal scientific name for the ancient aquatic arthropod *Hughmilleria socialis.* You might ask, "So what?" It is named after a man. You might still ask, "So what? Aren't a number of things named after per-sons?" But this name is unusual because it contains the *full* name of that person: Hugh Miller.

———

humanitarians   Remove a few letters from this word and scramble the rest. The appropriate result is "Samaritan."

Humuhumunukunukuapuaa   This word, which is the name for a small Hawaiian triggerfish, has the rare distinction of containing five palindromic parts—in other words, parts that read the same backward and forward. They are "humuh," "umu," "nukun," "uku," and "aa." The "apu" is the only non-palindromic part.

hurrah   This word comes from the sound of a cheer; it's onomatopoeic. The word first appeared in print in 1686.

hush   Some experts, including Wilfred Funk, have said that this is one of the ten most beautiful words in the English language.

husky   The husky dog may be husky in build, but the word has nothing to do with huskiness; it's simply a distortion of "Eskimo." Get it? Eskimo . . . Esky . . . hesky . . . husky.

Hygiene   Would you believe that this is an actual Colorado place-name?

hyperborean   This word may appear to mean "an extreme bore." In fact, it means "relating to an extreme northern region; frozen." It contains the same root seen in "boreal" (pertaining to the north wind).

hypersensitivity   This is probably the only English word in which you can find the letters that constitute "thirty-seven."

hypothesis   Father, on telephone: "Hello, son, this is your pa." Son's response: "Hypothesis your son."

I

IACOCCA   While this may be a prominent person's surname, it could once have been a very appropriate acronym: "I Am Chairman Of Chrysler Corporation of America."

iambi   This word begins and ends with *i*—a rarity! It is the plural of "iambus," a two-syllable element of a line of poetry.

icicles   What snowmen ride?

Idavada   Now, where do you suppose Idavada is located? Could it be on the Idaho-Nevada state line? Actually, yes!

idealize   Optical organs with twenty-twenty vision?

identified   Remove a few letters from this word and scramble the rest. The appropriate result is "defined."

idolater   The motto of a procrastinator?

illegal   Is this a sick bird?

impersonate   Remove a few letters from this word and scramble the rest. The appropriate result is "ape"—the verb, that is.

impregnate   Scramble the letters of "impregnate" and you have "permeating."

incompetents   Scramble the letters of this word and the appropriate result is "inept men cost."

incomprehensibles   Scramble the letters of this word and the appropriate result is "problems in Chinese."

incongruous   The Supreme Court judges the laws, but it is incongruous that the laws are made?

inconsiderate   Remove a few letters from "inconsiderate," and scramble the rest. You'll see what the word really means: "I don't care."

inconstitucionalissimamente   This is perhaps the longest word in the Portuguese language. It means "with the highest degree of unconstitutionality."

inconveniently   This is probably the only English word in which you can find the letters that constitute "ninety-nine."

Independents   Apparently the residents of Independence, Missouri, are independent-minded. For they do not call themselves Independencians, Independentians, or Independencers. Rather, they call themselves Independents.

Indianapolitans   Like the Annapolitans of Annapolis, the folks in Indianapolis use the "tan" ending and call themselves Indianapolitans rather than Indianapolisians or Indianapolisers.

indigestible   The gist of the meaning of this word is found simply by scrambling its letters—"gist: inedible"!

indivisibility   This is perhaps the longest common word in the English language having only one vowel, excluding *y*, that is repeated six times!

indomitableness   Scramble the letters of this word and the appropriate result is "endless ambition."

inefficiently   This is probably the shortest English word in which you can find the letters that constitute "fifty-nine."

infantry   A sapling—that is, a baby tree?

infer   If you have to be infer, which kind do you prefer—mink or muskrat?

ingratiate   Ingratiate, but when she finished eating, she changed from a gray dress to a red one. (See how long it takes you to figure out that pun.)

inning   This word has a phantom antonym—a phantonym: "outing," which isn't really the antonym of "inning" but looks as if it could be.

innominate   Scramble the letters of this word and the appropriate result is "no name in it."

innuendo   The boy hit the baseball so far that, unfortunately, it went innuendo!

insanable   This word may appear to mean "capable of becoming insane." In fact, it means "incurable." Its origin is related to that of the word "sanitary."

insatiable   Scramble the letters of "insatiable" and you have "banalities."

insect   You can transpose the third and fifth letters of this

---

73

word and come up with "incest." You can then transpose the first two letters of "incest" and get "nicest."

instinct   A dissatisfied guest said Holiday instinct and he'd never go back there. Somehow a skunk had gotten in.

insulate   Sometimes I come insulate from the office that it's already time to go back to work again.

insurgent   Scramble the letters of this word and the appropriate result is "unresting."

insurrectionist   Remove a few letters from this word and scramble the rest. The appropriate result is "incites riots."

intense   The days when most Native Americans lived intense are gone.

interchangeability   This is probably the only English word in which you can find the letters that constitute "thirty-nine," "eighty-nine," and "ninety-eight."

internecine   This is one of the few English words, if not the only English word, in which you can find the letters that constitute "nineteen."

intestines   Each and every letter of "intestines" appears twice, and only twice! This phenomenon is known as a pair isogram.

intolerable   If you remove a few letters from "intolerable" and scramble the rest, you'll discover that what is intolerable is usually "ill-borne."

intoxicate   Scramble the letters of this word and the appropriate result is "excitation."

intracistern   This word contains two six-letter words, one in the middle, and one on the outside: "racist" in the middle, and "intern" ("int" and "ern") on either end.

intrusion   This word defines itself when its letters are scrambled, for an intrusion "is to run in."

investigators   Scramble the letters of this word and you get the appropriate "great on visits."

ionization   This word begins and ends with "ion."

irreptitious   This word may appear to mean "free from repetition." In fact, it means "characterized by or resulting from an act of entering by stealth or inadvertence." The same major root is also found in the word "surreptitious."

irrorate   This may appear to mean "to make an error." In fact, it means "speckled." The word is also an obsolete verb meaning "to moisten."

Italian   Remove a few letters from this word and scramble the rest. The appropriate result is "Latin."

J

jäääärne This remarkable Estonian word has four consecutive appearances of the same vowel. It means "the edge of the ice."

Jacam This Canadian place-name comes from J. A. Campbell, probably one of the town's founders.

jazz In an August 1946 poll taken by the National Association of Teachers of Speech, this was named as one of the ten worst-sounding words in the English language.

jejunojejunostomy And you thought there were no four-*j* words! This is the name of a surgical procedure in which a passage is created between two portions of the jejunum, part of the small intestine.

Jernej This Yugoslavian forename begins and ends with *j*—a rarity!

Jerusalem The Holy City may be holy, but there is one thing, at least, that it actually has nothing to do with: the Jerusalem artichoke. The "Jerusalem" in "Jerusalem artichoke" is an English corruption of the Italian word for "sunflower," *girasole* (literally "sun circler": *Gira* means "circle," as in "gyroscope," and *sole* means "sun," as in "solar"). You see, the Jerusalem artichoke is a type of sunflower, which constantly turns toward the sun.

Jervaulx   You might never have guessed that this British place-name is pronounced "jarvis."

Joachimsdollar   To reflect its origin, the word "dollar" could have been "Joachimsdollar." Our word "dollar" comes from the end of the German *joachimstaler,* the name of a silver coin minted in Joachimstal. The *tal* part of the word probably meant "valley." So our word "dollar" may mean little more than "valley."

John Rhode   This is the appropriate pen name of the British author, Cecil John Charles Street. (Get it? "Street" equals "Rhode"!) Cecil Street (1884–1964) was a political writer, criminologist, and author of the Dr. Priestley detective novels of the 1920s and 1930s.

jokul   This word may appear to pertain to a little joke or to a yokel. In fact, it means "a mountain covered with ice and snow" in Iceland. It is related in origin to "icicle."

joviality   Another word for "joviality" is part of this word. It's "joy."

juicy   A more "sophisticated" use of this word: "Did juicy what I saw?"

jump   This word comes from the sound of someone jumping; it's onomatopoeic.

justify   A more "sophisticated" use of this word: "My ma promised me a quarter justify brush my teeth."

K

Kaaawa This word has three *a*'s in a row. It's the name of a town on the island of Oahu.

Kalamazoo Nowadays there's not much unusual about this word. Most people are familiar with the name of this city in Michigan. So why not make the name unusual again by adding a few more letters to it, so that it will be closer to its original name? Why not call it Kekekalakalamazoo, since the Indians originally called the valley there Ke-ke-kala-kala-mazoo, "where the water boils [or smokes] in the pot." Supposedly the name comes from a time when an Indian brave bet he could run to the river and back before a pot of water could boil.

Kanze This Indian tribe gave us the state name, Kansas. The spelling was a French one, and therefore the second *s* was not intended to be pronounced. Leave it to us Americans to pronounce "Kansas" as "Kansas"!

Katy This Texas place-name comes from the nickname of the Missouri, Kansas, and Texas Railroad.

kayak   This word is a palindrome; it reads the same way backward and forward.

Kellogg   If the famous manufacturer of cornflakes used the words that reflect the original meaning of the name, would as many people eat them? For a kellogg—the fourteenth-century spelling was "kelehoge"—was a butcher who specialized in killing hogs: kill hog!

Kensee   Guess on what state line this Kentucky city is located. Did you say Tennessee? Get it? *Ken*tucky and Tennes*see*.

Kenvir   Guess on what state line this Kentucky city is located. Virginia, of course!

kerosene   There was a time when, strictly speaking, we could not have legitimately written "kerosene" in this way. The word was originally a company's registered trademark, or brand name, and therefore required a capital letter and in some instances, a trademark symbol: Kerosene™.

kidnap   Is this child asleep?

Kilimanjaro   This name comes from the Swahili *kilima* (mountain) and *mjaro* (god of cold). Thus, Mount Kilimanjaro is Mount Mountain God of Cold.

Kim   In Korea, this is the most common surname.

kindred   Fear of relatives?

Kinnikinnik   This is one of the many spellings of the word for a mixture of sumac leaves and dogwood bark smoked by some peoples. We consider it the preferred spelling, though, because it reads the same way backward and forward.

---

kitty-come-down-the-lane-jump-up-and-kiss-me This is one of perhaps only three words in the English language having nine hyphens. It's the name of the cuckoopint, a European plant.

kleptomaniacs Scramble the letters of this word and you get what they do: "task policeman."

Klondike This river in the Yukon takes its name from an Indian word: *throndik,* meaning "river of fish." Thus "Klondike River" means "river of fish river."

knock This word comes from the sound of knocking; it's onomatopoeic.

Konica This name of the cameras manufactured by Konishiroku UK is a contraction of the words *"Konishiroku"* and *"ca*mera."

Kuikkjokk Five *k*'s in one word! This is the name of a town in Sweden.

KwEnihtEkot This mouthful, and eyeful, was the Algonkian Indian name for a river that ran through the state that took its name from that river's name. If it's of any help, the name meant "long tidal river." The river is the Connecticut River. And if you hadn't noticed, "Connecticut River" is a redundancy, meaning "long tidal river river."

L

La   Wouldn't this be a great name for a city in Virginia? La, VA—lava!

La Paz   This name of the capital of Bolivia is actually a truncated version of the real name bestowed on the city by the Spanish in 1548: Pueblo Nuevo de Nuestra Señora de la Paz (new town of Our Lady of Peace).

labioglossopharyngeal   This is one of the longest words beginning and ending with *l*.

laboratorial   This adjective contains two six-letter words: "orator" in the middle, and "labial" (pertaining to the lips) on the ends.

lambent   This word may appear to mean "pertaining to lambs." In fact, it means "flickering, bright, radiant."

Lamington   This New Jersey place-name sounds like a typical English place-name. In fact, though, it is not. The area was called "allametunk" (within-hills-at) by the Algonquin tribe living there. Soon "allametunk" became "Lametunk," then "Lamaton," and finally "Lamington."

---

lanolin There was a time when, strictly speaking, we could not have legitimately written "lanolin" this way. The word was originally a company's registered trademark, or brand name, and therefore required a capital letter and, sometimes, a trademark symbol: Lanolin™.

lariat This word originates from the Spanish *la reata* (the rope), So the next time you ask for a lariat—should the occasion ever arise—please don't say "the lariat"; that would be redundant. Instead, say, "Please pass the riat." Or, for Spanish speakers: "Please pass the *reata*." *Gracias!*

LASER This word is an acronym for *L*ight *A*mplification by the *S*timulated *E*mission of *R*adiation.

latchstring This word has made a name for itself by having six—count 'em, six—consonants in a row.

laundering Scramble the letters of this word and the appropriate result is "guard linen."

laundress The most appropriate women's attire for mowing the lawn?

Lawrence If you live in Lawrence, what do you call yourself? The residents of Lawrence, Massachusetts, call themselves Lawrencians, but the residents of Lawrence, Kansas, call themselves Lawrentians.

lawsuit A police officer's uniform?

Lazbuddie The name of this city in Texas was created from the nicknames of two local ranchers, D. L. "Laz" Green and A. "Buddie" Shirley.

laziness A more "sophisticated" use of this word: "It's no wonder baby doesn't get tired—he laziness crib all day."

Leeuwarden   This is the name of a Dutch town. However, one should hesitate to say that this is the correct spelling of that town. For, since 1046, it has had 225 different spellings.

Lego   The name of these toy building blocks and their manufacturer was devised in the 1930s for children's wooden toys built by a Danish carpenter named Kirk Christiansen, and comes from the Danish *leg godt,* meaning "play well."

lemons   This is one of the few fruit-words in the English language that, when scrambled, forms the name of another fruit: melons.

Leominster   This British place-name is pronounced "lemster."

leporine   This word may appear to mean "like a leper" or "like a leopard." In fact, it means "pertaining to or resembling a hare."

level   This word is a palindrome; it reads the same way backward and forward.

Levene   This is not only the surname of some persons descended from Levites (ancient Jewish priests), but also most likely the only real-word anagram of "eleven."

levitative   Ignore the first letter in this word, and see what's left: "evitative." It's not a real word, but it does read the same way backward and forward. (You knew there had to be some reason for its presence in this dictionary.)

levitatively   Ignore the last letter in this word and see what's left: "levitativel." It's not a real word, but it does read the same way backward and forward.

———

license Instinctive knowledge of when to tell the truth—and when not to?

life insurance Remove a few letters from this phrase and scramble the rest. The appropriate result is "a secure 'fini.' "

lillypilly This may not look like a very long word, but it is—for what it denotes. For here you are looking at the longest word constituted entirely of letters having extenders—in other words, letters that extend beyond the midline: the *y* and *p* extend below the midline; the *i,* with its dot, and the *l* extend above the midline. The word is the name for an Australian tree of hard, fine-grained wood.

limericks Scramble the letters of this word and the appropriate result is "slick rime."

limnophilous This word contains four consecutive letters in alphabetical order: *m, n, o,* and *p.* It means "living in freshwater ponds or marshes."

linoleum There was a time when, strictly speaking, we could not have legitimately written "linoleum" this way. The word was originally a company's registered trademark, a brand name, and therefore required a capital letter and sometimes a trademark symbol: Linoleum™.

listen If you are going to listen, you should be silent. How can you turn "listen" into "silent"? Scramble the letters of "listen," of course!

literate The highway is usually clean, though sometimes people literate with garbage.

littoral This word may appear to be a misspelling of "literal." In fact, it means "pertaining to the seashore."

---

liturate   This may appear to be an illiterate spelling of "literate." In fact, it is a biological term meaning "spotted."

locomotive   A ridiculous reason?

locus   Something derogatory said under one's breath?

logarithm   The back-and-forth motion of loggers as they saw trees?

Los Angeles   This place-name is actually a truncated version of the full name given by Spanish missionaries in 1781: El Pueblo de Nuestra Señora la Reina de los Angeles de la Porcióncula" (the City of Our Lady the Queen of the Angels of the Little Portion).

lounge   Two other words are hidden in this word. Take the first letter and then every other letter, and you'll get "lug." Now make another word out of what remains: "one."

loxolophodonts   This is one of the longest words using only *o* for its vowel. These now extinct mammals were roughly the size of elephants.

lubrications   Scramble the letters of this word and the appropriate result is "oil acts in rub."

Luling   This is not a misspelling of "lulling," as in "lulling one to sleep." It is the name of a city in Texas where Lu Ling was the owner of the local Chinese restaurant—honest!

lullaby   Two word experts, Wilfred Funk and Willard Espy, agreed that this word and one other word, "murmuring," were among the ten most beautiful words in the English language. They disagreed, however, on the other eight.

luminous   Some experts, including Wilfred Funk, have said that this is one of the ten most beautiful words in the English language.

luthern   This may appear to be a loose pronunciation of "Lutheran" or a word meaning "pertaining to Martin Luther." In fact, it means "dormer window."

Lympne   You might never have guessed that the name of this village in the British Isles is pronounced "lim."

M

ma'am This word is a palindrome; it reads the same way backward and forward.

MAGIC This is the acronym for the Motorola Automatically Generated Integrated Circuit.

Maine Shouldn't this state be called "the Mainland"? Early explorers referred to the area as "the maine" to distinguish between the islands and the mainland in that part of New England.

Malayalam This may be the longest palindrome listed in every major collegiate dictionary. It's the name of a language spoken in India.

malediction Man talk?

malism This may appear to be a male-related ism. In fact, it is the belief that the world is evil.

mamelon This may appear to be the name of a type of melon or mammal. In fact, it denotes a small rounded hill, especially of lava. It comes from the French word for "nipple."

A related word, "mamelière," was the name for a medieval armor plate used to protect the breasts.

Mancunian   Could you have guessed that a Mancunian is a resident of Manchester, England?

manslaughter   This is a crassly ironic word, for it takes little effort to see "man's laughter" inside it.

Manxman, Manxwoman   Could you have guessed that this is the word for a resident of the Isle of Man? Why don't they call themselves Maniacs?

marksman   A German banker?

marram   This word is a palindrome; it reads the same way backward and forward. It's an Australian beach grass.

marriage   Scramble the letters of this word and the result is "a grim era."

Martin   In France, this is the most common surname.

Masters   You've heard complaints about people nowadays not knowing how to use an apostrophe correctly (we saw two bathrooms labeled "mens" and "womens"). Well, apparently this has been going on for quite some time. The fact is that the surname Masters came from a medieval worker who was the master's servant. So why not put the apostrophe back, like so: Master's?

matches   Another word for "matches" is inside this word. It's "mate."

matrimony   Scramble the letters of this word and the appropriate result is "into my arm."

mattoid   This word may appear to pertain to the shape of a mat. In fact, it denotes a borderline psychopath.

mattress   Remove an *s* from this word and scramble the rest. The appropriate result is "rest mat."

Mayday   This distress signal has nothing to do with either the month or the Russian Revolution. The word originates from the French *m'aider*, meaning "help me." So instead of "Mayday," the call could be translated into English as "Aid me!"

mayonnaise   Reverse the first eight letters of this word (iannoyam); then reverse the rest (es). The result: I annoy Ames.

M'daywawkawntwawns   This is a five-*w* word. It's the name of a group of Dakota Indians and is more frequently spelled "Mdewakantons."

meandering   Some experts, including Willard Espy, have said that this word is one of the ten most beautiful words in the English language.

measured   Scramble the letters of this word and the appropriate result will be "made sure."

medallion   This word is "pregnant" with twins: "medal" and "lion."

Medmenham   You might never have guessed that this British place-name is pronounced "mednam."

meet-her-in-the-entry-kiss-her-in-the-buttery   This is one of perhaps only three words in the English language having nine hyphens. It's the name of a flower, a pansy.

---

melanoid This word may appear to pertain to the shape of a melon. In fact, it means "characterized by dark pigments."

mellifluous Some experts including Willard Espy, have said that this is one of the ten most beautiful words in the English language.

melodious Don't make too much noise removing the *m, e, o, i,* and *s* from this word and then shuffling what remains. You just might end up with "loud."

melody Some experts, including Wilfred Funk, have said that this is one of the ten most beautiful words in the English language.

melomaniac This may appear to be the word for an easy-going (mellow) maniac. In fact, a melomaniac is a music lover or someone who is inordinately affected by music. "Melody" is related in origin.

Melusa Moolson This exotic-looking name was the pen name of Samuel Solomon (1904–1988), the India-born poet, judge, translator, and nonfiction author who wrote *The Saint and Satan* in 1930. Can you figure out why he chose that pen name? Hint: Anagram! Anagram! Anagram!

mendacious This may appear to pertain to something that has been well mended. Actually, it means "dishonest."

menology This may appear to mean "the study of men." In fact, it is an ecclesiastical calendar of saints' days. "Menopause" contains the same "men" root, which means "month." "Logy" pertains to "word" *(logos),* not "study."

merciful What happens when you mix up "merciful" and throw out a few letters? You get "cruel."

---

meretricious This may appear to mean "that which is characterized by merit (meritorious)." In fact, it means "gaudy, cheaply ornamental, or after the manner of a prostitute" (a meretrix is a prostitute). Actually "merit," "meretricious," and "meretrix" are all related, having their origin in a Latin verb meaning "to earn" or "to gain."

mesial This word may appear to pertain to something that is menial and measly. In fact, it means "in or directed toward the middle."

messuage This may appear to be a misspelling of "message." In fact, it is a legal term for a house and its adjacent buildings.

metaphysics Remove a few letters from this word and scramble the rest. The mysterious result is "mystics."

metromania This may appear to pertain to people with an excessive love for the city (metropolis) or for urban mass transit (the Metro). In fact, it means "an excessive enthusiasm for writing verse." It is related in origin to "meter" and "measure."

Michael East This is the opposite-direction pen name of the Australian novelist Morris West, who wrote *The Devil's Advocate* (1959) and *The Shoes of the Fisherman* (1963).

midnight Scramble the letters of this word and the appropriate result is "dim thing."

midshipman Scramble the letters of this word and the appropriate result is "mind his map."

migraine This word could have been "hemigraine," for it comes from the Greek *hemikrana,* from *hemi,* meaning "half," as in "hemisphere," and *kranion*, meaning "the upper part of the head," as in "cranium." In a sense, the word "migraine" represents only half of "hemi"—that is, half of half. So is a migraine actually only a *quarter* of the upper part of the head?

milestone   You can transpose the first and third letters of this word and come up with another word: "limestone."

militarism   The best way to defeat militarism is to scramble its letters. For when you do so, you reveal that "I limit arms."

milk of magnesia   There was a time when, strictly speaking, we could not have legitimately written this phrase in this way. It was originally a company's registered trademark, a brand name, and therefore required a capital letter and, in some instances, a trademark symbol: Milk of Magnesia™.

milliner   The origin of this word has nothing to do with mills, in the sense of hats being made in mills. The word originates from "Milaner," a native or inhabitant of Milan. It seems that Milan was known for its fancy goods and apparel; so the Milaner became closely associated with millinery—Milanery, that is.

Mills   You've heard complaints about people nowadays not knowing how to use an apostrophe correctly. Well, apparently this has been going on for quite some time. The fact is that the surname Mills came from a medieval worker who was the miller's servant. So you might say that everyone whose name is Mills could be called Miller's!

mimeograph   There was a time when, strictly speaking, we could not have legitimately written this word in this way. It was originally a company's registered trademark, a brand name, and therefore required a capital letter and, in some uses, a trademark symbol: Mimeograph™.

miniate This word may appear to mean "small." In fact, it means "to paint red," and it once referred especially to some letters in an illuminated manuscript. Actually, "miniature" and "miniate" are closely related in origin. For "miniatures" were small, predominantly red paintings. "Miniature" soon became the word for a small version of anything, not just a picture.

miniature A more "sophisticated" use of this word: Take a sedative, and you'll fall asleep the miniature in bed.

minim This word is a palindrome; it reads the same way backward and forward. A minim is a musical term meaning "half note."

minister Scramble the letters of this word. The appropriate result is "sin timer."

Minneapolitans This is what residents of Minneapolis call themselves—like the Annapolitans of Annapolis and the Indianapolitans of Indianapolis.

Minnehahapolis If Minneapolis is a contraction of the Indian word *minnehaha* (falling water) and the Greek word *polis* (city), then is its full name Minnehahapolis?

Minolta This brand name is an acronym of *M*achine, *IN*strument, *O*pitca*l*, and *TA*jima. Tajima is part of the name of a Japanese wholesale firm, Takima Shoten, which deals in silk fabrics. It is run by the father of Kazuo Tashima, the founder of the Minolta Camera Company.

---

minutes Remove the "sun" from "minutes," shuffle what's left, and you'll get "time."

mirage Scramble the letters of this word and the appropriate result is "imager."

misfortune Remove half the letters in "misfortune," and you'll end up with the appropriate result: "ruins."

misinterpretations Scramble the letters of this word and the appropriate result will be "one interprets amiss."

misnomer This is a word for something that is inaptly named or labeled. Since the word itself means, literally, "misnamed"—from *mis* plus *nom* (name), it is obviously a word that has been named appropriately; in other words, "misnomer" is a good name for a word that means "something inaptly named." Thus, "misnomer" is *not* a misnomer; it is quite appropriately named. Got that?

Mississippi As much trouble as many people have spelling this state name, the fact is that it originally didn't have even one *s* in it. For the word is a French spelling—they apparently liked *s*'s—of the Chippewa word for "large river": *mici-zibi.*

missive This word may appear to pertain to something missed or missing. In fact, a missive is a letter, often a formal or official one. It is ultimately related in origin to "missile," as both letters and missiles are sent out.

mist Some experts, including Wilfred Funk, have said that this is one of the ten most beautiful words in the English language.

mob In the seventeenth century the common people, or rabble, were said to be "mobile" because they were considered fickle and easily moved. "Mobile" soon went out of style, though, and was shortened to "mob." People are fickle, you know.

mobility The probability that a small crowd will develop into an angry mob?

moderated Three other words are hidden in this word. Take the first letter and then every third letter, and you'll get "met." Now find another word by taking every third letter starting with the *o*: "ore." And finally, find still another word by taking every third letter starting with the *d*: "dad."

modulation Scramble the letters of this word and the appropriate result is "I am not loud."

Moneysterling This London place-name has nothing to do with either money or sterling. It comes from the Irish *Monasterlym*, meaning "the monastery of O'Lynn."

Montevideo If folklore is to be believed, this place-name may have originated from a sort of rebus, words or syllables represented by means of pictures. It is claimed that the name originates from a Portuguese mapmaker's notation pertaining to a mountain located at Montevideo. The notation supposedly read "monte VI de O," indicating that this was the sixth mountain from the west: *monte* means "mountain"; VI, of course, is Roman numeral six; and the *o* stood for *oeste*, meaning "west," in Portuguese. In fact, it is more probable that the name comes from the Portuguese *Monte vidi eo*, meaning "I saw the mountain."

moo This is not only the word (or, as we like to say, the coward) for the sound a cow makes. It is also the appropriate acronym for the Milkbottles Only Organization.

---

moonlight Scramble the letters of this word and the appropriate result is "thin gloom."

Mooselookmeguntic This name of a lake in Maine may be the longest American place-name. It is an Indian word that means roughly, "where the hunters watch the moose at night."

moralize You can never have too many friends speaking in your defense. The moralize, the better!

Morocco How many people know, or remember, that Marrakesh is the second largest city in Morocco? It is especially ironic that people have trouble remembering that Marrakesh is in Morocco. For in fact "Morocco" is actually a Spanish corruption of "Marrakesh."

Moscow Did you know that Moscow was named for a man named Moscoso and that the city was originally supposed to be called Mosco, but the *w* was added by mistake! Well, that's true, but only for the city of Moscow, Kansas!

Motswana Could you have guessed that this was the word for a resident of Botswana? And guess what the word for the residents (plural) of Botswana is: Botswana!

Mount Hope Bay If you ever go to Mount Hope Bay, in Massachusetts and Rhode Island, you may be struck by the absence of any mountains or large hills—that is, anything that might suggest to the name of the bay. You might wonder whether the name came from the residents' hope that there would one day be a mountain there. In fact, though the name was not supposed to be Mount anything! It appears that the Narragansett tribes may have originally called the area "montop," meaning "uncertain." "Montop" became "Mount Hope."

Mousehole The name of this town in Britain is pronounced "moozel."

mumble This word comes from the sound of a mumble; it's onomatopoeic.

mumpsimus This word may appear to be what one is called who has the mumps. In fact, it means "a bigoted adherent to exposed but customary errors." It is said that the word originates from a popular story about a priest who mistakenly said "mumpsimus" instead of "sumpsimus" (the Latin word for "we have taken") when conducting the mass. The priest stubbornly repeated the error even after having been corrected.

murdrum This word is a palindrome; it reads the same way backward and forward. A murdrum was a fine collected under the Norman kings of England for the offense of murder.

murmur This word comes from the sound of a murmur; it's onomatopoeic.

murmuring Two word experts, Wilfred Funk and Willard Espy, agreed that this word and one other word, "lullaby," were among the ten most beautiful words in the English language. They disagreed, however, on the other eight.

Muscoidea This word has all the vowels, each of which appears only once and in reverse alphabetical order. The word is the name of a superfamily of insects to which the common housefly belongs.

mutter This word comes from the sound of muttering; it's onomatopoeic.

muttering Scramble the letters of this word and the appropriate result is "emit grunt."

———

muvaffakiyetsizliklerimizdendirki   Speakers of Turkish probably see nothing particularly unusual about the size of this word. The Turkish language uses a word-forming process known as agglutination, in which smaller words are added to one another to form other words of virtually unlimited length. This word, for example, translates into "It is because of our failures that . . ." As they say, "Muvaffakiyetsizliklerimizdendirki we English speakers have great difficulty speaking Turkish."

mystacial   This word may appear to mean "related to mystical things." In fact, it means "having a fringe of hairs suggestive of a mustache."

mysticize   The bullet fortunately mysticize and merely grazed his forehead?

N

Nabisco This is an acronym of *N*ational *Bisc*uit *Co*mpany, formed in the United States in 1898. In 1901, the name was registered, and in 1971 the company name became Nabisco Inc.

namby-pamby This cute rhyming word actually originates from a gentleman named *Amb*rose Philips.

Natasha Read this word backward and you get "ah, Satan." Big deal, huh? Well, did you know that the word that means "little Natasha" is "Natalie"? And what do you suppose "Natasha" means? It means "Christmas child"! Quite a contrast, huh? By the way, "Santa," when rearranged, can spell "Satan."

nausea You might think that you were simply coming up with a clever pun if you said that "nausea" is a "nauing (gnawing) feeling at sea"—in other words seasickness. In fact, though, your pun would reflect exactly what "nausea" originally meant: seasickness. The word comes from the Greek *nausia,* "seasickness." The "nau" element appears in other sea-related words such as *"nau*tical" and *"nau*machy" (sea battle).

negation Scramble the letters of this word and the appropriate result is "get a no in."

nerd Why must someone who doesn't happen to be cool and who doesn't dress fashionably be saddled with a label like "nerd"? Have we no decency? When will this name-calling end? Don't people realize that it is simply *wrong* to call someone a nerd? After all, some maintain that the word "nerd" comes from the name of Edgar Bergen's puppet, Mortimer Snerd. So call them "snerds"!

Nescafé This brand name comes from the name Henri Nestlé and the French word for "coffee," *café*. Made in Vevey, Switzerland, Nescafé became, in 1938, the first brand of instant coffee.

news Somehow this word, which looks like (and is, in its origin) a plural, came to be regarded as a singular. We say, for example, "What *is* the news today?"—not "What are the news today?" Yet it was not always that way: "And wherefore should these good news Make me sicke?" (Shakespeare, *2 Henry IV*, iv, 2 [1623]).

nickname Do you have any extra names lying around? An "ekename," meaning roughly "extra, or added, name," was what a nickname was originally called. But when people heard "an ekename," they thought they were hearing "a nickname." You might say that the nickname for "ekename" stuck, and so we now call an ekename a "nickname."

Nigeria Nigeria may be in the "dark" continent, and its inhabitants may have "black" skin, but the word "Nigeria" has nothing to do with either the Spanish term for "black," *negro,* or the Latin term for "black," *niger.* Rather, the name is taken from one of its chief rivers, the Niger, which gets its name from *gher n-gherea,* meaning "river among rivers."

NIIOMTPLABOPARMBETZHELBETRABSBOMONIMONKONOT-DTEKHSTROMONT This is the longest acronym in any language. It is an English transliteration of a Russian acronym for the following (translated into English): the Laboratory for Shuttering, Reinforcement, Concrete and Ferroconcrete Operations for Composite-monolithic and Monolithic Constructions of the Department of the Technology of Building-Assembly Operations of the Scientific Research Institute of the Organization for Building Mechanization and Technical Aid of the Academy of Building and Architecture of the USSR.

Nile If you refer to the Nile as either "the Nile River" or "the river Nile," you're saying the same thing twice. And you're saying not only the *same* thing but also an *odd* thing. For "Nile" originates probably from the Semitic-Hamitic *nagal,* which meant "river." So whether you say "river Nile" or "Nile River," you're still saying "river river."

Ninety-Six Guess what? This is not only a number but also a South Carolina place-name. But what else would you call the place? Apparently the people couldn't figure out a name for their settlement, which was ninety-six miles from Fort Prince George on the Keowee River. So they picked a number.

niobium Problem: you're chemist and you extract a new element from a mineral ore called tantalite. What do you call this element? Well, tantalite was named after the god of Greek myth, Tantalus, and Tantalus's daughter was named Niobe, and the element is an "offspring" of tantalite. . . . Need we say more?

nitrate The best deal for long-distance calling?

nocent This may appear to mean "penniless." In fact, it means "hurtful" or "harmful."

nodose This may sound like the name of a brand of caffeine pill. In fact, it means "knotty," or "knobbed."

NOISE This is the appropriate acronym for the National Organization to Insure a Sound-Controlled Environment! (Sorry about the loud terminal punctuation; we should have used a simple period.)

noisome This may appear to have something to do with noise, but in fact it means "harmful, unwholesome, disgusting, especially to the sense of smell." It is related in origin to "annoy" but not to "noise."

Nome Nome takes its name from a note made on a chart of the coastal region of Alaska by an English mapmaker. The note was misread as "Nome." What, you might ask, did the note actually say? It said "?name," for the mapmaker did not know the name of that place. But by *not* knowing the name, he gave Nome its name.

nominate Scramble the letters of this word and you get "a mention."

nonintervention Five *n*'s!

nonannouncement There may be no other word in the English language that contains six *n*'s.

nonuniformitarian This is one of the longest words beginning and ending with *n*.

Nora Read this feminine name backward and you get a male name—specifically "a Ron."

Norfolk Unlike the cities in Virginia and Massachusetts, which take their names from Norfolk, England, the "Norfolk" in Nebraska is a corruption of "north fork."

Norfolkers Since we are from Norfolk, Virginia, we wish to ask why we can't call ourselves Norfolkers. In fact, the people of Norfolk, Virginia, are called Norfolkians. People in Norfolk, Nebraska, are called Norfolkans, and people in Norfolk County, England, are called North Anglians. Are there any Norfolkers?

Normal Would you believe that this is the name of a town in Illinois?

nosology This word may appear to pertain to the study of noses. In fact, it is the term for a branch of medicine dealing with the classification of diseases. *Nos* is a Latinate root meaning "disease."

nostalgia Scramble the letters of this word and the appropriate result is "lost again."

notable This word is "pregnant" with two sets of twins: "not" and "able," and "no" and "table."

nowhere This is one of the few words that can be split in such a way as to suggest the opposite meaning of the original word. "Nowhere" can be split to form "now here." Yet if something is now here, it certainly is *not* nowhere.

nuclear You can transpose the first two letters of this word and come up with "unclear."

nursery In 1933 a Hollywood studio banned this word from all its films because it was considered "unsuitable."

Nutsville Nutsville is an actual place people live in. It's in Virginia. Now you know where all the nutty people really *do* come from!

---

nylon This synthetic fiber is protected by a patent, but its name is not a trademark. The word "nylon" was coined in 1938 by the Du Pont Company as a generic name and appears to have been merely an invention with no particular rationale, though its ending, at least, might have been inspired by "rayon," which came before it. Although many attempts have been made to explain the significance of the "nyl" element, they have been generally unsuccessful. The most common suggestion is that the element comes from *New York* and *London.* While the letters may have been arbitrarily chosen, they do suggest the word "vinyl." But there is no vinyl in nylon.

O

obediency You can remove the two *e*'s, the *i*, and the *y* from this word and you'll still have obediency—obdnc, that is!

obstinate Take "no" away from "obstinate," and shuffle the remaining letters. The result describes an obstinate person (and one who says "no" a lot): "a bit set."

occision This may appear to be a misspelling of "occasion," but actually it's a real word meaning "slaughter." It is related in origin to "in*cision*," "homi*cide*," and other words pertaining to cutting or killing.

ocellated This may appear to be a misspelling of "oscillated," but actually it's a real word meaning "resembling eyes." It is related in origin to "bin*ocul*ar" and other words pertaining to eyes.

Oeaei This all-vowel word is the Egyptian name for the wife of Ra-amen, the spondist of Pthah.

Ofcookogona This is part of the formal scientific name for a millipede, the *Ofcookogona alia.* You might ask, "So what?"

This millipede is named after a man. You might still ask, "So what? Aren't a number of things named after persons?" Yes, but this name contains the person's first and middle initials as well as his surname: O. F. Cook.

offense The best way to separate your property from your neighbor's is to put up offense?

often This word is "pregnant" with twins: "of" and "ten."

Ogopogo This word is a palindrome; it reads the same way backward and forward. Ogopogo is the name of a mythical monster of Okanagan Lake in British Columbia, Canada.

okonoko This is a palindrome; it reads the same way backward and forward. Okonoko is the name of a West Virginia village on the Maryland state line.

oniomania This may appear to mean "an irrational love of onions," but actually it's an uncontrollable urge to buy things. The word originates from the Greek *onios*, "to be bought."

onomatopoeia Some experts, including Willard Espy, have said that this is one of the ten most beautiful words in the English language. Appropriate, I suppose, for a word that denotes the use of words that sound as they sound because of the sound that they sound like. (Isn't that a nice-sounding sentence?)

orange Would you like a norange? No, that's not a misprint. Or at least it didn't used to be. "Orange" was originally "norange," but people thought the first *n* was part of the article "an," so "a norange" became "an orange."

Ordinary Would you believe that people actually live in Ordinary, Virginia?

orgulous This word may appear to be related to "orgies." In fact, it means "proud" or "haughty."

oronooko A rare five-*o* word! It's the name of a type of tobacco.

osculate This may appear to be a misspelling of "oscillate," but actually it's a real word meaning "to kiss." It is related to the Latin *osculum,* meaning "little mouth."

ottetto This word is a palindrome; it reads the same way backward and forward. *"Ottetto"* is Italian for "octet."

ouch This word comes from the sound of a common response to pain; it's onomatopoeic. "Ouch" joins "atchoo" as one of the rare examples of a word that people often use even though it does not actually represent the exact sound one would naturally make. For example, usually when something hurts, you might exclaim "ohooo!" or "owww!" But since the word "ouch" has become so well established as the word that represents that general response, we often actually say "ouch" when something hurts. "Ouch" has had a long history, first appearing in print in 1654!

Ouija The Ouija (WEE-jee) board supposedly answers one's questions (with "yes," for example). The board is, in fact, quite aptly named: "Ouija" is a hybrid of the French word (*oui*) and the German word (*ja*) for "yes."

outlanderish *See* "etaoin shrdlu."

Ovaltine Originally marketed as Ovalmaltine, this malt drink took its name from the Latin word for "egg" *(ovum),* plus "malt" and the suffix "ine." Because the name was difficult to register in Britain, it was shortened to "Ovaltine." The product was marketed by Dr. George Wander in Berne, Switzerland.

Ovens   The name of this village in County Cork, Ireland, is pronounced "oovan."

overstudious   This word contains four letters in alphabetical order; *r, s, t,* and *u.*

overtired   Does this mean "having too many tires on your car"?

ovoviviparous   A great *v* word to say! It means "producing eggs that develop inside the body and hatch within or immediately after expulsion from the parent." From *ovo* (egg) plus *vivi* (live) plus *parous* (relating to bearing children).

owelty   This may appear to mean "the condition of being an owl," but actually it's another word for "equality."

Oxonian   Could you have guessed that an Oxonian is a resident of Oxford, England?

oyer   This may appear to be a word for something that causes someone to say "Oy, vey!" But actually an oyer is a criminal trial. The word ultimately originates from the Old French *oir* (to hear), which is from the Latin *audire*. After all, a trial is a hearing.

P

pacifical Ignore the first and last letters in this word, and see what's left: "acifica." It's not a real word, but it does read the same way backward and forward. You knew there had to be some reason for its presence in this dictionary.

pacificatory Three other words are hidden in this word. Take the first letter and then every third letter, and you'll get "pico" (a peak, a conical mountain). Now find another word composed of every third letter, starting with the *a:* "afar." And finally, find still another word by taking every third letter, starting with the *c:* "city."

palamate This word may appear to mean "a good friend," but actually it means "web-footed." It is related to "palm."

palindromes By now you probably are aware that palindromes are words that read the same way backward and forward. This word does *not* read the same way in reverse, so "palindromes" is not a palindrome! Yet "palindromes," read backward, is "semordnilap"—a word that forms a different word when read backward. And remember, a semordnilap is not a palindrome (though some will say that is a *type* of palindrome), since the word formed when read backward is a *dif-*

ferent word, not the same word. Now everything should be crystal clear. Right? If so, you may wish to refer to the "sentence" and "semordnilap" entries in this dictionary to help muddy things up again.

But wait, we're not yet finished with this word. It seems that "palindromes" is a bigger word than you might think. How big is it? Glad you asked. It is so big that it has seven French cities and eight Italian cities embedded in it. Just scramble the word up and presto violà! The French cities are Paris, LeMans, Amiens, Orleans, Laon, Sedan, and Prades. The Italian cities are Rome (or Roma), Milan (or Milano), Naples (or Napoli), Palermo, Pisa, Salerno, Siena, and San Remo.

Palmolive This brand name comes from the palm and olive oils contained in the soap first manufactured by B. J. Johnson in Milwaukee in 1898.

pantaloonery Four other words are hidden in this word. Take the first letter and then every fourth letter, and you'll get "pan." Now find another word by taking every fourth letter, starting with the first *a*: "ale." Find a third word by taking every fourth letter, starting with the first *n*: "nor." And finally, find still another word by taking every fourth letter, starting with the *t*: "toy."

panties Scramble the letters of this word and you get "a step-in."

Papanicolaou It was George Papanicolaou for whom the Papanicolaou Smear Test was named. You probably know it better as simply the Pap smear.

parables Scramble the letters of this word and you get "able raps."

PARADISE This word also happens to be the wondrous acronym for Phased Array Radars and Diverse Integrated Semiconductor Elements. Could it also be defined as "what one needs to play many board games"?

---

paramelaconites Five other words are hidden in this word. Take the first letter and then every fifth letter, and you'll get "pen." Now find another word by taking every fifth letter starting with the first *a*: "Ali." And find another word by taking every fifth letter starting with the *r*: "rat." And still further, find another word by taking every fifth letter starting with the second *a*: "ace." And finally, find still another word by taking every fifth letter starting with the *m*: "mos" (the singular of "mores"). By the way paramelaconites are tetragonal minerals.

parasites Binoculars?

parental This word can be scrambled to form two other words that also relate to parenthood—and they both start with *p*: "prenatal" and "paternal."

parenthesis Scramble the letters of this word and the appropriate result is "phrase set in."

parishionership This is one of the longest words that begins and ends with *p*.

parrot This word is "pregnant" with twins: "par" and "rot."

Parsons You've heard complaints about people not knowing how to use an apostrophe correctly. Well, apparently this has been going on for quite some time, for the name Parsons came from a medieval parson's servant. So why not put the apostrophe back, like so: Parson's?

partitioned It is only with trepidation that you should go about undoing that which is partitioned. For if you scramble the letters in "partitioned," the result might be "trepidation."

Pasadena Legend has it that this place-name is an abbreviation, but no one is certain what it's an abbreviation of. Supposedly the name was concocted in 1875 from four Indian words that ended in "pa," "sa," "de," and "na." The four words may have meant "crown of the valley" or perhaps "key of the ranch."

PASSION   This is the acronym for the Program for Algebraic Sequences, Specifically of Input-Output Nature. Could anything sound less passionate?

pasteurize   That runner is so fast that he goes pasteurize before you can even get a glimpse of him.

pat   This simple-looking word has the rare distinction of meaning the same thing whether its read backward or forward, even though the word formed in reverse is a different word, "tap."

pat   This word comes from the sound of a pat; it's onomatopoeic.

pathologist   A Boy Scout?

patronessship   Three *s*'s in a row.

pattern   This word is "pregnant with twins: "pat" and "tern."

paucity   An urban center greatly in need of economic growth?

Peculiar   Would you believe that people actually live in Peculiar, Missouri?

Peen   Wouldn't this be a great name for a city in Utah? Peen, UT—peanut.

peepeye   This may be the only word in the English language that, when read in reverse, forms another word whose syllables are pronounced the same, but in reverse order: "eyepeep."

---

peeweep This word is a palindrome; it reads the same way backward and forward. "Peeweep" is the English name for the greenfinch and the lapwing.

Pentagon What you do with a name tag?

penthouse There was no "house" in the original Middle English word for "penthouse," *pentis*. The word is ultimately related to "appendage."

Pepsi-Cola This brand name was coined in 1898 by North Carolina drugstore manager Caleb D. Bradham. He patterned his elixir after Coca-*Cola* and hoped it would relieve dys*pepsi*a (indigestion).

Pepsodent Elida Gibbs coined the name of this toothpaste from "*pepp*ermint" and *dent,* from the Latin word for "tooth" as in "*dent*ist").

Perdue This English surname comes from the Norman-French oath *Per Dieu! Per Dieu* (By God! By God!).

perimeter Another word for "perimeter" is inside this word. It's "rim."

perpetuity If you ever find yourself with a typewriter whose keys don't work except for the top row of letters (*qwertyuiop*), and if you need to type " perpetuity," consider yourself fortunate. "Perpetuity" is one of the longest words you can type without using any keys except those in the top row of letters.

pessimal This obscure word is actually the antonym of a more familiar word, "optimal." "Pessimal" means "the *worst* possible situation or condition."

pettitoes This may appear to be a misspelling of "potatoes," but actually it's a real word for "feet" or "edible pig's feet."

You're probably saying, "Of course, 'petite toes,' " but in fact, the word is related ultimately to the French *petite oye* (small goose).

phantomnation   This word has appeared in a number of "legitimate" dictionaries. Webster's once defined it as "appearance, as of a phantom; illusion (obsolete and rare)." Rare! Obsolete! I'll say! In fact, this word is so rare and so obsolete that it may never have been used, except of course in some dictionaries. The first dictionary (or dictionary supplement) to include it was entitled *Philology on the English Language,* published in 1820 by Richard Paul Jodrell. It seems that Mr. Jodrell tended to combine words without using hyphens. So he misquoted the source of this supposed word, citing the following passage from the *Odyssey*: "These solemn vows and holy offerings paid/ To all the phantomnations of the dead" (x, 627). In actuality, there was no such solid word as "phantomnations." It was two words: "phantom nations." And you thought dictionaries included words that people used.

phlegmatic   In an August 1946 poll taken by the National Association of Teachers of Speech, this word was recognized as one of the ten worst-sounding words in the English language. It means "having a sluggish or stolid temperament."

Phoenicians   Yes, Phoenicians are alive even today! But they're all in Phoenix, Arizona.

phyllophyllin   If you're right-handed and you can type, you'll discover that this may be one of your favorite words (left-handers, see "tesseradecades"). "Phyllophyllin" is one of the longest words containing only letters that are located on the three rows of the keyboard designed to be typed by the right-hand. The word is the name of a bluish-red biochemical pigment.

PICASSO   This is an acronym for Pen Input to Computer And Scanned Screen Output.

piloerection   This may appear to pertain to pile-driving or erecting pile, but actually it's a word for an involuntary erection or bristling of hairs in response to cold, shock, or fright. The "pil" part of this word is related in origin to the hair-like carpet "piles."

ping   This word comes from the sound of something pinging; it's onomatopoeic.

pioneer   Remove a few letters from this word and scramble the rest. The appropriate result is "opener."

pirates   Scramble the letters of this word and the appropriate result will be "sea trip."

PISCES   This is an acronym for Production Information Stocks and Cost Enquiry System.

Pitt   The surname of William Pitt the Elder, first earl of Chatham (1709–1778), may have contributed to more American place-names than any other surname. All of the following places are named after this English statesman, political leader, and defender of the American colonies before the Revolutionary War: Pitt County, North Carolina; Pittsburgh and East Pittsburgh, Pennsylvania; Pittsburg County, Oklahoma; Pittsburg, California (and Kansas); West Pittsburg, California; Pittsfield, Illinois (and Massachusetts and New Hampshire); Pittston, and West Pittston, Pennsylvania; Pittsylvania County, Virginia; Chatom, Alabama; four cities named Chatham; Chatham County, Georgia (and North Carolina); and Chatham Strait, Alaska.

pittance   Scramble the letters of this word and the appropriate result is "a cent tip."

---

planet If a planet is indeed a star, then why is it not called a star? Does "planet" mean "star"? Actually, "planet" is all that remains of the original Greek phrase *asteres planetai,* meaning "wandering stars." The "aster" part is, of course, the "star" root, as in "asteroid." The "planet" part is related to "wandering." So if you speak of a planet, you're really talking about "a wandering," without any indication of *what* is wandering—a star, that is.

Plaska This city in Texas was named for an early settler named Pulaski. So why is it called Plaska? Well, quite simply, it seems that the post office mistakenly spelled it that way.

playmate Read the first three letters of this word backward (alp); now read the rest backward (etamy). Result: Al, pet Amy!

pleasure This word is "pregnant" with twins: "plea" and "sure."

plop This word comes from the sound of a plop; it's onomatopoeic.

plowshare Scramble the letters of this word and the appropriate result is "helps a row."

plump In an August 1946 poll taken by the National Association of Teachers of Speech, this word was recognized as one of the ten worst-sounding words in the English language.

plutocrat In an August 1946 poll taken by the National Association of Teachers of Speech, this word was recognized as one of the ten worst-sounding words in the English language. It means "one who exercises power by virtue of wealth."

pneumonoultramicroscopicsilicovolcanoconiosis This very long word is the name of a respiratory disease that occurs especially in miners.

poachers   Scramble the letters of this word and the appropriate result is "cop hares."

point   When people talk about something being "beside the point," they are using an expression that actually has its origins in the sport of archery, where arrows can miss the "point," or mark. "Point," incidentally, defines itself when every other letter in it is read backward and forward. Read every other letter, and you get "on." Then read every other letter in reverse, and you get "tip." Result: "on tip." (We used the phrase "backward and forward" here. It would have been more accurate to have said "forward and backward," but we were afraid you might say that such wording sounds funny. And after all, we wouldn't want to be unidiomatic. By the way, why is it that people say "back and forth" instead of "forth and back"? Usually people go forward before they decide to go backward, don't they?)

POLAND   This is not the name of a country—well, not always. It is, sometimes, an acronym used in the military in love letters: Please Open Lovingly And Never Destroy.

pollicitation   This may appear to be the word for a citation given by a police officer, but actually it's a civil law term for an unaccepted offer.

polytechnical   Pet owner: "Polly wanna cracker or a nickel?" Parakeet: "Polytechnical!"

Pontrefact   You might never have guessed that this British place-name is pronounced "pomfret."

pop   This word comes from the sound of something popping; it's onomatopoeic.

populate   What son tells tardy father?

portrait   Bad habit?

---

possessor Ignore the first and last letters in this word, and see what's left: "ossesso." It's not a real word, but it does read the same way backward and forward. You knew there had to be some reason for its inclusion in this dictionary.

postneuralgic This is a particularly long example of a word in which no letter is repeated. This phenomenon is sometimes called an isogram.

postponed Take "no" away from "postponed," and shuffle the remaining letters. The result describes what something is that is postponed: "stopped."

pound As a unit of measurment, this word has been so shortened that, taken literally, it no longer means anything more than "weight." "Pound" is actually the end part of a Latin phrase, *libra pondo,* meaning "a pound (*libra*) by weight (*pondo*)." The "libra" was the actual unit of measurment. "Pondo" merely indicated that something was being weighed. So if you ask someone what something weighs and he tells you "a pound," he is in reality telling you nothing more than that it does have weight—big news!

precaution Scramble the letters of this word and the appropriate result is "I put on care."

precipitevolissimevolmente This is perhaps the longest word in the Italian language. It means "as fast as possible."

predestination Scramble the letters of this word and the appropriate result is "I pertain to ends."

Preet Wouldn't this be a great name for a city in Indiana? Preet, Ind.—pretend!

---

prelate   Is this an oxymoron? Is this the word for someone who comes before (pre) everyone else and yet is late?

premature   Read the first letter of this word; then read the rest backward (erutamer). Result: Peru-tamer—a sobriquet for Francisco Pizarro?

premeditation   Remove the "ita" from "premeditation" and scramble what's left. The result is "ponder time."

premorse   This may appear to be the word for a feeling one has before feeling remorse, but it's actually an adjective meaning "abruptly terminated as if broken off," as in "a premorse root."

preposterous   This preposterous word means literally "with the front behind."

Presbyterians   Scramble this word and you get a phrase that might well describe Presbyterians: "best in prayers."

preservation   Remove a few letters from this word and scramble the rest. The appropriate result is "save it."

preservative   Remove a few letters from this word and scramble the rest. The appropriate result is "ever save."

priesthood   This word is a hybrid: "priest" is of Latin origin; "hood" is of Anglo-Saxon origin.

Primghar   This Iowa city takes its name from *eight* persons! The commissioners who laid out the town were *P*umphrey, *R*oberts, *I*nman, *M*cCormack, *G*reen, *H*ays, *A*lbright, and *R*enck. You know we wouldn't make up something like that.

primitivistic   This is one of the longest words using only the letter *i* for its vowel.

----

proficiencies This word breaks the spelling rule, "*i* before *e*, except when preceded by a *c*"—and breaks it twice.

promise Scramble "promise" and you have "imposer." Scramble it again and you have "semipro."

proofreaders Remove a few letters from this word and scramble the rest. The appropriate result is what proofreaders find: "errors."

prophage This word may appear to be related to prophesying. It might even appear to be a collective term for prophecies. But actually it refers to a protective bacterial virus that is harmless to its host.

propose Scramble the letters of "propose" and you have "opposer."

prosecute Another word for "prosecute" is inside this word. It's "sue."

protein Scramble the letters of "protein" and you have "pointer."

Pseudopunctipennis psedopunctipennis This is a remarkable tautonym: a word or phrase that repeats itself. Why? Who knows? This is the name of a malaria-carrying mosquito.

psst! This word comes from the sound of someone's "psst"; it's onomatopoeic.

pungent Male wordplay artist?

punishment Scramble this word, and you'll get a punishment—"nine thumps."

---

pupils Read this word backward and you get "slipup." Wordsmiths call such a word a semordnilap, a word that forms a different word when read backward.

purchasing Scramble the letters of this word and the appropriate result is "ring up cash."

Puu Huluhulu This is one of the longest words using only the *u* for its vowel. It's the name of a mountain in the southern part of the island of Hawaii.

pycnic (or pyknic) This word looks and sounds like "picnic," but it means "short, stocky, and muscular."

Pyrenees The name of this mountain range that divides France from Spain probably originates from either the Basque *pyren* or the Celtic *byrin,* both of which mean "mountain." Thus, the Pyrenees Mountains are the Mountain Mountains!

Q

Qaraqalpaq This word begins and ends with *q* and has the distinction of having three *q*'s, not one of which precedes a *u*. It's the name of a Turkish people of Central Asia.

Qawiqsaqq A four-*q* word! It's the name of a bluff in Alaska.

quack This word comes from the sound of a duck quacking; it's onomatopoeic.

Quaouiatonon This gem was the original name of a tribe of Indians whose name later became Ouaouia. It means, roughly, "one who puts to sleep," possibly alluding to the Indians' ability to hypnotize people. Big deal, you say. "Ouaouia," however, gave us the name of the state in which these Indians lived. For Ouaouia changed again . . . to Iowa.

Quelea quelea quelea This remarkable tautonym (a word or phrase that repeats itself) repeats itself three times. It's the scientific name for the African weaverbird.

queue This is the only word in the English language that retains its pronunciation even when its last four letters are dropped!

queueing   This word has five vowels in a row.

quodlibetary   This word has all the vowels, including *y,* each of which, except *y,* appears only once and in reverse alphabetical order. It means "an argument over a technical point."

quodliteral   This is one of the longest English words in which each of the vowels appears once and in reverse alphabetical order. It means "having four letters."

R

RACE   This is the appropriate acronym for the Rochester (New York) Area Commuter Express.

radar   This word is a palindrome; it reads the same way backward and forward.

raincoats   What rain wears in the winter?

raisin bran   There was a time when, strictly speaking, we could not have legitimately written this phrase in this way, for it was originally a company's registered trademark, or brand name, and therefore required a capital letter and, sometimes, a trademark symbol: Raisin Bran™.

ramate   This may appear to mean "like a ram." In fact, it means "having branches."

Ramona   Read this feminine name backward and you get a male name: "an Omar."

rampage   Another word for "rampage" is inside this word. It's "rage."

ransom   I walked most of the way but I ransom too?

raptorial   This may appear to describe an eloquent rap song, as in "He waxed raptorial," but actually it means "living on prey" or "adapted to seize prey."

rationalize   What realization will you come to when you scramble the letters in "rationalize"? "Realization"!

rattle   This word comes from the sound of something rattling; it's onomatopoeic.

Ratus ratus ratus   This remarkable tautonym (a word or phrase that repeats itself) actually repeats itself three times. Can you guess what it's the scientific name of? Could it be the common rat? Yes!

razzmatazz   Four *z*'s in one word!

Reagain   This is not a redundant word meaning "do over again," but an Irish nickname meaning "little chieftain." We know it better as the surname Reagan.

realistic   Scramble the letters of this word and the appropriate result is "it is clear."

rearrange   An extra stove for the back of the house?

rebarbative   This may appear to refer to the taking of another barbituate, but actually it means "serving or tending to repel." The word is related to "barber," "barb," and other words pertaining to hair, beards, and similar things that may be long and stiff.

recordership   This word contains two six-letter words, "orders" from the middle, and "rechip" from the ends.

redder This word is a palindrome; it reads the same way backward and forward.

reentered Each *e* in this word is pronounced differently!

refer This word is palindrome; it reads the same way backward and forward.

regulate Another word for "regulate is inside the word. It's "rule."

reindeer Why not call this animal a "reindeerdeer" or even "reindeerreindeerdeer?" You say that would be ridiculous, do you? Well the fact is that "rein" comes from Old Norse "hreinn," which means (did you guess?) "reindeer." So maybe we should just call it a "rein."

reinstall The place where reindeer are housed?

reknit Read this word backward and you get "tinker." Wordsmiths call such a word a semordnilap, a word that forms a different word when read backward.

remacadamizing This is one of the few words in any language that incorporates roots from five different sources: *re* is Latin; *mac* is Celtic; *adam* is Hebraic; *iz* is Greek; and *ing* is Anglo-Saxon! The word pertains to a road-paving process named after its developer, McAdam. (For more on McAdam, see the "Tarmac" entry.)

Remlap The city of Remlap, Alabama, was named after the local railroad station. Why, you might ask, was the station called Remlap? Well, it got its name from a local family, the Palmers. And how did "Palmer" begat "Remlap"? Do you have to ask?

---

repaid Read this word backward and you get "diaper." Wordsmiths call such a word a semordnilap, a word that forms a different word when read backward.

repaper This word is a palindrome; it reads the same way backward and forward.

REPEET This may be a misspelling of "repeat," but it is also the somewhat appropriate acronym for Reusable Engines, Partially External Expendable Tankage.

repertoire If you ever find yourself using a typewriter whose keys don't work except for the top row of letters (*qwertyuiop*), and if you need to type "repertoire," consider yourself fortunate. For "repertoire" is one of the longest words you can type without using any other keys.

Republican Is there any significance in the fact that most of the letters in the word "Republican" can be rearranged to form the word "incurable"—or that "Democratic," scrambled, forms "rated comic"?

reredos This may appear to be what you would call those things that you do after you've already redone them. In fact, however, a reredos is a screen or partition wall behind an altar. The word is related in origin to "rear" and "dorsal."

rescue Scramble the letters of this word and the appropriate result is "secure."

RESISTORS This is one of the greatest acronyms of modern times: Radically Emphatic Students Interested in Science, Technology, and Other Research Studies.

respite Another word for "respite" is inside this word. It's "rest."

---

restores   This word begins and ends with "res."

retentiveness   This is one of the few English words, if not the only English word, in which you can find the letters that constitute "seventeen."

retinopathy   This word, which denotes a noninflammatory disease of the retina, is probably the shortest English word in which you can find the letters that constitute "thirty-one."

reuniter   Ignore the first letter of this word, read the remainder in reverse, and what do you get? "Retinue."

reviver   This word is a palindrome; it reads the same way backward and forward.

Revlon   This brand name comes from the names Charles *Rev*son, the founder of Revlon International Corporation, and Charles *L*achman, one of his partners.

revolution   If you remove a few letters from "revolution" and then toss around the letters that remain, you just might have to get "violent."

Richmond   If you live in Richmond, what do you call yourself? The residents of Richmond, Virginia, call themselves "Richmonders," but the residents of Richmond, California, and Richmond, Indiana, call themselves "Richmondites."

ridiculous   Remove an *i* from this word and scramble the rest. The appropriate result is "ludicrous."

ring   This word comes from the sound of ringing; it's onomatopoeic.

riroriro   If you want to know what a gray warbler, the small songbird of New Zealand, sounds like, this word will give you some idea. "Riroriro" is another name for the gray warbler. This marvelous word contains four *r*'s and it's a great example of onomatopoeia.

roar   This word comes from the sound of a roar; it's onomatopoeic.

roborant   This may appear to denote the angry sound of a robot. However, it means "an invigorating drug or tonic." The word is related in origin to "robust."

Rochester   If you live in Rochester, what do you call yourself? The residents of Rochester, Indiana, call themselves "Rochesterites," but the residents of Rochester, New York, call themselves "Rochesterians."

Rochesterville   You've heard of Rochester, New York, and you probably assume that Rochesterville is a different city. But in fact for five years, Rochester was Rochesterville. In 1817 the place was named Rochesterville after Colonel Nathaniel Rochester. In 1822, the "ville" was dropped.

rotatively   Ignore the last letter of this word, read the remainder in reverse, and what do you get? "Levitator."

rotator   This word is a palindrome; it reads the same backward and forward.

routine   Remove a few letters from this word and scramble the rest. The appropriate result is "one rut."

Roystonea   This is part of the formal scientific name for a palm, the *Roystonea regina*. You might ask, "So what?" But this palm is named after a man. You might still ask, "So what? Aren't a number of things named after persons?" But this name contains the full name of that person: Roy Stone!

---

rugby   A bee indigenous to shaggy carpets?

runagate   This may appear to denote a driver who has run through a gate. In fact, however, it is simply another word for a renegade, fugitive, or vagabond.

Russia   Did you know that Russia is in Ohio? Indeed, it's the name of a city in Ohio.

Rx   This is a sort of word and a sort of abbreviation. In reality, though, the *x* shouldn't be there. For although "Rx" is, in a sense, an abbreviation for "prescription," it actually represents an *R* with a slash through its tail, which was an abbreviation for "recipe." "Recipe" was a form of the Latin *recipere,* "to take, receive," as in "receipt." It was usually the first word in prescriptions—as they directed one to *take* a certain quantity of medicine. Although in medical usage "recipe" ultimately became "Rx," the word has remained in common usage as a way of referring to a prescription—that is, a formula or directions—for preparing certain foods.

S

S No, this wasn't always just a letter of the alphabet. It once was someone's name: the middle name of Harry S Truman! No, the *S* didn't have a period after it, and it wasn't an initial. Unlike virtually every other word with an *s* in it, however, this *S* was pronounced "ess," not "sss." (Note, however, that today most major sources include a period.)

Saab The name of this car comes from the initials of the *S*venska *A*eroplan *A*ktie*b*olaget (Swedish Aeroplane Company), founded in 1937.

sable What politicians often do in their speeches?

sabulous This may appear to be a contraction for "simply fabulous" or perhaps a word meaning "pertaining to sable." It is neither. In fact, it means "sandy."

SAFE This is the ironic acronym for the San Andreas Fault Experiment.

sagas This word is a palindrome; it reads the same way backward and forward.

Sahara This name comes from the Arabic word "sahr," meaning "desert." To speak of the Sahara Desert, therefore, is to speak of the "Desert Desert."

sainted It does make a difference where you put the *t* in this word. For if you move it to the second position, "sainted" will become quite the opposite: "stained."

saippuakauppias This marvelous palindrome which reads the same way backward and forward, is not an English word—big surprise! It's the Finnish word for "soap dealer."

sali Wouldn't this combining form meaning "salt" be a great name for a city in Virginia? Sali, VA—saliva!

Salinan What do you call someone who lives in Salina, Kansas? Yes, a Salinan. But what do you call someone who lives in Salina*s*, California? Yes, a Salinan, too. But why not a "Salinization"?

Salopian Could you have guessed that this is the word for a resident of Shropshire, England? Rather sloppy, don't you think?

SAMANTHA This is an acronym for the *S*ystem for the *A*utomated *Man*agement of *T*ext from a *H*ierarchical *A*rrangement.

samlet This may appear to mean "little Sam." But it actually means "a young salmon."

sample It is not mere coincidence that "sample" and "example" are extremely close in meaning. Indeed, it seems that somewhere along the line, the *e* sound dropped out of "example" and the word became "sample." In fact, in Old English, "sample" was spelled "asaumple." Its ultimate origin: Latin *exemplum*!

Santa   Do you know what lingers inside Santa? Just scramble the word. Could it be . . . *Satan?*

sap   In an August 1946 poll taken by the National Association of Teachers of Speech, this word was recognized as one of the ten worst-sounding words in the English language.

Sarben   In the search for a good name for their city, some folks have gone to great lengths . . . and some haven't. To come up with their city's name, the folks in Sarben, Nebraska, looked no further than the name of the state: Nebraska = Nebras = . . . need we say more?

Satan   This is not just the name of the prince of darkness. It's also an acronym for Speed And Throttle Automatic Network!

Saugonian   Could you have guessed that a Saugonian is a resident of Saugus, Massachusetts? Well, if the people in Halifax, Nova Scotia, can call themselves Haligonians, then why not?

sawbwas   This word is a palindrome; it reads the same way backward and forward. The sawbwas were ruling princes of Mongoloid tribes in Burma.

Saybrook   This Connecticut city was not named for any local brook. In fact, it is probably the first coined name of an American city, named in 1635 for two patent holders, Lord Say and Lord Brooke.

sciurine   This may appear to be the name of a type of urine, but actually it means "pertaining to squirrels."

seamstress   Here's a sexist word. Can't a man be a seamstress? No, he's called a tailor. But can't a woman be called a

---
137

tailor? You might suggest, "Why not call a man tailor a seam-ster?" Well, there's a problem still, because the "ess" at the end of "seamstress" is actually redundant, since "seamster" was the original word for a woman tailor. A seamstress, then, is technically a "female female tailor"—a very female tailor? In fact, the man tailor was originally called simply a "seamer," one who sewed seams. So there you have it. We have two choices: either call everyone, man or woman, a tailor (or a seamer), or call the men seamers and the women seamstresses or, to be more traditional, seamsters.

SEARCH   This is the appropriate acronym for the System for Electronic Analysis and Retrieval of Criminal Histories.

seat   This simple word is one of the few from which you can remove any letter and still have a word.

seclusion   Scramble the letters of this word and the appropriate result is "close us in."

sedentes   This seldom used plural is actually the antonym of a fairly common word, "migrants." Migrants move from place to place; sedentes remain in one place.

seize   This word is noteworthy for one major reason: it's a fairly long computer word. When it's written in block-style capital letters and turned upside down, it forms computer-style numbers. "SEIZE" turned upside down becomes 32135.

self-centeredness   This is one of the longest words using only the letter *e* for its vowel.

semaphore   Scramble the letters of this word and the appropriate result is "see arm hop."

semitimes   This rare word is a palindrome; it reads the same way backward and forward. It means "half-times."

semordnilap   Here's a word that is not only "semordnilap" but also a semordni!ap. Does that make sense? You see, a semordnilap is a word that, when read backward, forms a different word. When you read "semordnilap" in reverse you get "palindromes" (see the "palindromes" entry). This word is also autological, but that's another story. Autological words are defined under "word" in this dictionary.

Semple   This name is actually a shortened form of the French "St. Paul." The English were quick to adopt—and adapt—the language of the French-speaking Normans who conquered Britain in 1066. The *t* was dropped, and few people now realize that the remaining *S* represented "saint." Occasionally "St." loses its *t*. Rarely, however, does it lose its *S*. For a rare example, see "tawdry," below.

Sensodyne   This toothpaste is so called because of its power (*dyne*) to eliminate the *sens*itivity of the teeth. The "dyne" ending is unusual for a pharmaceutical product but fairly common for mechanical and electrical devices such as Rotodyne.

sensuousness   Ignore the last letter in this word, and see what's left: "sensuousnes." It's not a real word, but it does read the same way backward and forward. (You knew there had to be some reason for its inclusion in this dictionary).

sentence   This word is not a sentence, though it is quite clearly "sentence." Furthermore, this "sentence" is a word, not a sentence. To put it in simple language, what we're dealing with here is a heterological word. . . . Oh, sorry, perhaps it's not simple . . . Things that are heterological do *not* refer to what they are. So since the word "sentence" is *not* a sentence, it's heterological. Okay?

separation Scramble the letters of this word and the appropriate result is "one is apart."

sequoia This is one of the shortest English words in which each the vowels appears only once, and four of the vowels appear back-to-back.

Seroco This city in North Dakota is named for none other than *Se*ars *Ro*ebuck and *Co*mpany. Really!

SESAME This is the appropriate acronym for Supermarket Electronic Scanning for Automatic Merchandise Entry.

set This word is not as simple as it seems. As a noun it has fifty-eight different meanings and uses, and as a verb, 126 different meanings and uses.

Seymour This name is actually a shortened form of the French "St. Maur." The English were quick to adopt—and adapt—the language of the French-speaking Normans who conquered Britain in 1066. The *t* was dropped, and few people now realize that the remaining *S* represented "saint." Occasionally "St." loses its *t*, but only rarely does it lose its *S*. For a rare example, see "tawdry," below.

shahs This word is a palindrome; it reads the same backward and forward.

shameful This word looks as if it should mean the opposite of "shameless," but in fact, of course, it means the same.

shamrock Fake diamond?

Shanghai Did you know that Shanghai is in Virginia? It is!

shanghaiings Each and every letter of "shanghaiings" appears twice, and only twice. This phenomenon is known as a pair isogram.

Shenandoah Some experts, including Willard Espy, say that this is one of the ten most beautiful words in the English language.

sherbet A horse that can't lose?

shittim This word isn't nasty at all. It refers to the wood of the shittah, a tree mentioned in the Bible.

shoe Before your very eyes, this word will become another word if you simply move the first letter to the end. Move the *s* to the end, and you get "hoes." Notice also that the sound of the word has changed completely.

shoplifter Remove a few letters from this word and scramble the rest. The result denotes what a shoplifter does: "pilfers."

shredded wheat There was a time then, strictly speaking, we could not have legitimately written this phrase in this way. The phrase was originally a company's registered trademark, a brand name, and therefore required a capital letter and, sometimes, a trademark symbol: Shredded Wheat™.

shrimp Were short people first derogatorily called shrimps because they were as short as the tiny marine crustaceans? Or were the tiny marine crustaceans first called "shrimps" because they were as short as the people? If you answered no to the first question and yes to the second question, you're right! It was only after the derogatory term for short people ("shrimps") developed that the shrimp in the sea got their name.

shrimp scampi   "Shrimp" in this phrase is redundant, for "scampi" means "shrimps."

shrubbery   Scramble the letters of this word and the appropriate result is "berry bush."

siccative   This may appear to mean "sickening," but actually it means "promoting water loss." The word is related to "desiccate" (to dry up).

sideburns   There are no burns on the side of the face of someone who has sideburns—only hair. The word "sideburns" was taken from Ambrose Burnside, the famous Civil War general who wore the distinctive burnsides—oops—sideburns.

Sidney   This name is actually a shortened form of the French "St. Denis." The English were quick to adopt—and adapt—the language of the French-speaking Normans who conquered Britain in 1066. The *t* was dropped, and few people now realize that the remaining *S* represented "saint." Occasionally "St." loses its *t*, but only rarely does it lose its S. For a rare example, see "tawdry," below.

siffilate   This may appear to mean "causing syphilis," but actually it means "to whisper."

significant   This word is "pregnant" with quadruplets: "sign," "if," "I," and "can't."

similarly   Three other words are hidden in this word. Take the first letter and then every third letter, and you'll get "sir." Now take every third letter starting with the *i*: "ill." And finally find still another word using every third letter starting with the *m*: "may."

sinned Read this word in reverse and you get "Dennis." Wordsmiths call such a word a semordnilap, a word that forms a different word when read backward.

sitophobia This may appear to mean "fear of sitting." Actually, though, it denotes a fear of eating. The word is related in origin to "para*site*."

Situh Wouldn't this be a great name for a city in Delaware? Situh, Del.—citadel!

skeleton There is actually nothing left of the original phrase from which the word "skeleton" originates that describes what a skeleton is. The word is only half of the original Greek phrase *skeletòn sôma* (dried-up body). *Sôma*, meaning "body," also appears, for example, in "psychosomatic" and "chromosome;" *skeletòn* means simply "dried-up." The bones that make up a "skeleton" are what's left of a body, not what's left of a "dried-up." Yet we call the heap of bones a "skeleton," not a "soma" (or even a "body"). Oh, well.

Skilligallee This odd U.S. place-name comes from *Ile aux Galets*, a French term. To the non-French settlers, *Ile aux Galets* sounded like "Skilligallee."

skua This short word has the rare, and obscure, distinction of having a meaning related to the meaning of the word formed when this word is read in reverse: auks. Both "auks" and "skua" are northern seabirds.

SLAM Is there any question about what the Ship-Launched Antiaircraft Missile can do? Its acronym is "slam."

---

slanderous   Scramble the letters of this word and the appropriate result is "done as slur."

Smackover   French trappers and hunters from Louisiana described the area in Arkansas now known as Smackover as *sumac-couvert*, meaning "sumac-covered," because of the multitude of sumac bushes that grew there. *Sumac-couvert* sounded like Smackover, whatever that means. There's more than one version of this story, however. It is also maintained that "Smackover" came from *Chemin-couvert*, a French term for "road-covered"—possibly an allusion to a stream arched over by branches at that location. In either case, "Smackover" doesn't seem to be the best translation.

SMART   Who could question the Supervisors Methods Analysis Review Technique, the acronym for which is SMART?

sneeze   It may sound funny, but "sneeze" was once "fneeze!" The Middle English "fnesan," meaning "sneeze," somehow became "sneeze." Some speculate that the script *f* was misread as an *s*. Others speculate that the *f* was gradually dropped, perhaps because it's easier to say "nee" than "fnee," and that the *s* was later added to it, since "sneeze" resembled other nose-related words such as "snore," "snort," and "snot." "Fneeze," though, has the advantage of being a lot funnier sounding, and, after all, sneezing is kind of fnuny—er, funny—don't you think?

snicker   This word comes from the sound of someone snickering; it's onomatopoeic.

snore   This word comes from the sound of someone snoring; it's onomatopoeic.

snort   This word comes from the sound of a snort; it's onomatopoeic.

sob This word comes from the sound of a sob; it's onomatopoeic.

soccer "Soccer" originated as students' slang for Association Football. In a sense, all that is left of its original name is the "soc" part of "association." What if the collegians had instead borrowed from the middle of "football?" Would the game be known today as "otber"—or "ooter?"

softheartedness Scramble the letters of this word and the appropriate result is "often sheds tears."

soldierly Scramble the letters of this word and the appropriate result is "so ye drill."

sophomore This word means literally "wise fool."

SORDID This is the appropriately sordid acronym for the Summary Of Reported Defects, Incidents and Delays!

South Sea Islands Remove an *s* from this place-name and scramble the rest. The appropriate result is "a thousand isles."

Southleight Would you have guessed that the British place-name is pronounced "sowlee?"

sovereign Remove a few letters from this word and scramble the rest. The appropriate result is "I govern."

spectacle Is this another word for "housecleaning?" Tackling specks of dust?

Spectacular There's at least one place in New York that *no one* can deny is spectacular: Spectacular, New York.

---

spectators   Scramble the letters of this word and the appropriate result is "actors' pets."

spit   This word comes from the sound of spitting; it's onomatopoeic.

splotches   Another word for "splotches" is inside this word. It's "spots."

spoons   Read this word backward and you get "snoops." Wordsmiths call such a word a semordnilap, a word that forms a different word when read in reverse.

sputter   This word comes from the sound of something sputtering; it's onomatopoeic.

squeak   This word comes from the sound of a squeak; it's onomatopoeic.

stable   Before your very eyes, this word will become two other words if you gradually move the first letter to the end. Move the *s* to the end and you get "tables." Now move the first letter of this new word to the end and you get "ablest." The agility is remarkable, isn't it?

stallion   This word is "pregnant" with twins: "stall" and "ion."

state   This simple-looking word has the rare distinction of meaning the same thing whether it's read backward or forward, even though the word formed in reverse is a different word: *etats*, a French word meaning—you guessed it—"states."

stenographer   Remove a few letters from this word and scramble the rest. The appropriate result is "page noter."

stepfather   "Step" relations—stepfather, stepmother, and so on—did not get their names from steps in the sense of positions or steps, in family trees or family relationships. Rather, this prefix comes from the Old English *steop*, which in turn comes from a Germanic root meaning "bereave." When someone is bereft of his or her spouse and remarries, the new spouse becomes a stepparent—a bereaved parent—to any children from the previous marriage.

stinkhorn   This word isn't at all as nasty as it sounds. Actually, it's the name of a type of fungus.

strengths   The *e* in this word is indeed very strong, for this is the longest word with only one vowel.

stripe   Before your very eyes, this word will become other words if you gradually move the first letter to the end. For instance, move the *s* to the end, and you get "tripes." Now move the first letter of this new word to the end, and you get "ripest."

subcontinental   This is one of the longest English words containing one appearance of each vowel in reverse alphabetical order.

sublet   A small submarine?

submarine   Scramble the letters of this word and the appropriate result is "buries man."

sufficiencies   This word breaks the spelling rule, "*i* before *e* except after *c*"—and breaks it twice.

suggestion   Scramble the letters of this word and the appropriate result is "it eggs us on."

Sulah   Wouldn't this be a great name for a city in Maine? Sulah, ME—salami!

sulphonphtaleins   This chemical term is the longest word in the English language that contains one appearance only of each vowel.

sunbeams   Structural elements that hold the sun up in the sky?

sunglasses   What the sun wears in order to see better?

superextraordinarismo   This is perhaps the longest word in the Spanish language. It means "extraordinary."

supervisor   A great pair of glasses?

surgeon   Scramble the letters of this word and you get what the surgeon says: "Go, nurse."

surrebutter   This may appear to be a type of butter, but actually it denotes the reply in common law pleading of a plaintiff to a defendant's rebutter.

sweet-toothed   This hyphenated word contains three consecutive pairs of letters!

swims   Write this word out in longhand, then turn the paper upside down, and it still says "swims."

swish   This word comes from the sound of a swish; it's onomatopoeic.

swoosh   This word comes from the sound of a swoosh; it's onomatopoeic.

synopsis   Read the first part of this word backward: "ponys"; now read the rest backward: "sis." The result: pony's sis.

T

tambourine Remove a few letters from this word and scramble the rest. The appropriate result is "beat."

tangent After spending several hours in the sun, he's now quite a tangent?

Tangerine What do you call the fruit that grows in Tangier, Morocco? Right, a tangerine. What do you call a resident of Tangier? Yes, a Tangerine!

tantrums Scramble this word, and you'll discover that people who throw tantrums "must rant."

tarmac Tarmac is a binder for surfacing roads, airport runways, and parking areas. It comes indirectly from the surname of John Loudon McAdam (1756–1836), a Scottish inventor and engineer who was general surveyor of English roads from 1827. It is to McAdam that we owe the words "macadam," "macadamize," and "remacadamizing," since he introduced the process of paving roads by laying and compacting several layers of broken stone. The name "Tarmac" was later coined by E. Purnell Hooley, the county surveyor of Nottingham who, in 1901, discovered by chance a process for further improving roads. When he noticed a patch of road near an ironworks in Denby, Derbyshire, that was completely dustless and unrutted by traffic, he investigated. He discovered that the road had accidentally been covered with tar when a barrel tipped over. To remedy the situation, workers covered the tar with blast-furnace slag from the nearby ironworks. So inspired was Hooley by the result that in April 1902 he obtained a patent for a method of mixing slag with tar. He called the mixture Tarmac. The "mac" was an allusion to the macadamizing process.

Tarquin Fintimlinbinwhinbimlin Bus Stop-F'Tang-F'Tang-Ole-Biscuit Barrel   This is the legally changed name of Britisher John Desmond Lewis, a member of Cambridge's Raving Looney Society. Ah, to be loony!

Taumatawhakatangihangakoauauotamateaturipukakapiki-maungahoronukupokaiwhenuakitanatahu   This is the longest place-name currently in use in the world. The name designates a hill in New Zealand. In Maori, it translates as "the place where Tamatea, the man with the big knees, who slid, climbed, and swallowed mountains, known as Landeater, played his flute to his loved one."

tawdry   This word could have been "stawdry" or even "sawdry." But this is a rare etymological case of a saint losing her *s*. It seems that the seventh-century queen of Northumbria, St. Audrey, was fond of wearing necklaces, and when she died of a throat tumor it was presumed that the tumor was punishment for that fondness. In commemoration of the saint, a kind of silk necktie called "Seynt Audries lace" was sold at a special fair. The presumably tawdry (cheap and showy) tie ultimately gave to us the word "tawdry," which is essentially "S*t. Audrey*" without the *S*. It is usually the *t,* not the *s,* that disappears from *St.* See, for example, "Semple," above.

teammate   Each and every letter of "teammate" appears twice, and only twice. This phenomenon is known as a pair isogram.

Technicolor This is a blend of "*techn*ical *color*," a process dating from 1917, when the Technicolor Motion Picture Corporation produced the first Technicolor film, *The Gulf Between*.

Teddymore This Mississippi place-name is an Americanization of *tête-de-morte* (death's head).

tedious You can remove all the vowels from this word and you'll still have tedious—tds, that is!

Teflon This is a contraction of the chemical name for a tough, heat-resistant resin: poly*tetrafluo*roethyle*ne*. The chemical was first produced by Du Pont in 1938. Just think, it could have been called Potrath, Oyfutyl, Lyfleth, Trurot, or any of a thousand other possible combinations. (But Trurot was probably not a leading contender.)

teheeing This silly-looking word—a form of "tehee" (to titter)—may be the only anagram of "eighteen."

television This twentieth-century word is a hybrid: its prefix is of Greek origin, and its suffix is of Latin origin.

Tenino Allegedly, railroad men who went through this tiny village in Washington during the Depression called it Ten-Nine-Oh, from which it got its name. Actually, though, the name is Chinook for "fork" or "junction."

terror-stirring This hyphenated word should strike terror in those who swore there were no five-*r* words in English.

Tesnus The name of this city in Texas is simply "sunset" written backward.

tesseradecades If you're left-handed and you can type, this may be one of your favorite words, along with "after-cataracts," for "tesseradecades" is one of the longest words containing only letters that are typed by the left hand. The word means "groups of fourteen."

Texahoma Where do you suppose Texahoma is located? Could it be on the border between Texas and Oklahoma? Actually, yes!

the centenarians Scramble the letters of this phrase and the appropriate result is "I can hear ten tens."

Theda Bara Why did Theodosia Goodman take this stage name? It is an anagram of "Arab death."

theriacal This may appear to be a misspelling of "theatrical," but actually it's a word meaning "medicinal."

thermos Not so long ago the word "thermos" required a capital *t* because it was a trade name. Today the word is usually not capitalized, and any company can manufacture a thermos and call it a thermos.

Thorney This is the name of an island in Britain. It means "thorn island," the "ey" ending being Old English for "island." The problem is that today it is called Thorney Island. So it appears that Thorney Island is "Thorn Island Island!"

three This word is rarer than you might think, for one can scramble the letters and form two different words, both having identical meanings. They are "heter" and "rehte," both of which mean "severe" or "cruel."

3M One of the few words consisting of a number and a letter, this brand name comes from the three initial *m*'s of Minnesota Mining and Manufacturing Company, the original company name.

thrid No, this is not a misspelling of "third." It is actually a very *old* spelling of "third," dating back to the twelfth century. After all, the old spelling made sense: the word is related to "three," not "theer" or "thir." Yet by the linguistic process known as metathesis, the *r* and *i* sounds gradually were inverted, so that by 1175 "thrid" had become "therdde." And no one has ever put it back the way it started.

thriteen   No, this is not a misspelling of "thirteen." It is, rather, a very old spelling of "thirteen." By the year 1200, "thrittene" was the accepted spelling. After all, it made sense: the word is related to "three" not "theer" or "thir." Yet, again, by the linguistic process known as metathesis, the *r* and *i* sounds gradually were inverted, so that by 1398 "thrittene" had become "thyrtene."

thrity   No, this is not a misspelling of "thirty." (You should have gotten the idea by now. But theer times—er, three times—should do the trick.) It is, rather, a very old spelling of "thirty." Before the year 1350, "thritti" was the accepted spelling. After all, it made sense: the word is related to "three," not "theer" or "thir." Yet by the linguistic process known as metathesis, the *r* and *i* sounds gradually were inverted (sounds familiar, doesn't it?), so that soon "thritti" became "thurtty."

throb   This word comes from the sound of something throbbing; it's onomatopoeic.

thud   This word comes from the sound of a thud; it's onomatopoeic.

thunderbolt   The kind of lock used on a storm door?

thyrotoxicosis   This medical term is probably the shortest English word in which you can find the letters that constitute "thirty-six."

Ti   This Oklahoma place-name was created simply by reversing the initials of "Indian Territory."

tiffy   This adjective meaning "peevish" has at least one claim to fame: it may be the only real-word anagram of "fifty."

---

tirade The female version of a panty raid?

tirade An air pump?

toupee Toupee—but the third one gets in free?

together This word is "pregnant" with triplets: "to," "get," and "her."

toilet A little toy?

tolerant There were two ants of unequal size. One was a tol-erant than the other!

tollway A tollway, of course, is a place for automobiles. Read the word backward, though, and you'll get "yawl-lot." And what is a yawl-lot? It's a place for boats!

Tomato Would you believe that people actually live in Tomato, Arkansas?

TOPCOPS This is the appropriate acronym for The Ottawa (Canada) Police Computerized On-line Processing System.

toreador This word is "pregnant" with triplets: "to," "read," and "or."

Torpenhow The name of this hill in Britain is a conglomer-ation of *tor,* which means "hill"; *pen,* which means "hill"; and *how,* which means—you guessed it—"hill." So it is literally "hill hill hill," right? Well, not quite. You see, its full name is Torpenhow Hill!

Toshiba This trademark is a contraction of the firm's full name, the *To*kyo *Shiba*ura Electric Company, named after the region of Tokyo where the firm's headquarters is located.

tradesmen Scramble the letters of this word and the appro-priate result is "need marts."

---

trampoline This word used to be a trade name. Today of course the name is in the public domain, and a trampoline can be any trampoline, whether or not it was produced by the original company that held the trademark.

tranquil Some experts, including Wilfred Funk, have said that this is one of the ten most beautiful words in the English language.

transubstantiationalist This is one of the longest words beginning and ending with *t*.

treachery In an August 1946 poll taken by the National Association of Teachers of Speech, this was recognized as one of the ten worst-sounding words in the English language.

tribulation Remove a few letters from this word and scramble the rest. The appropriate result is "trial."

Troglodytes troglodytes This remarkable tautonym (a word or phrase that repeats itself) is the scientific name of a small English wren.

Trojans Will it come as a great surprise to you that the residents of Troy, New York, are called Trojans? Well, they are, you know!

trolley Reverse the positions of the last two letters of this word and you get the purpose of a trolley: "t' roll ye."

trophic This word may appear to mean "pertaining to trophies." Actually it means "nutritional."

troubador Remove a few letters from this word and scramble the rest. The appropriate result is "bard."

troubles Remove a few letters from this word and scramble the rest. The appropriate result is "blues."

truancies Two other words are hidden in this word. Take the first letter and then every other letter, and you'll get "Tunis." Now make another word out of what remains, using every other letter, starting with the *r*: "race."

trustworthiness Scramble the letters of this word and the appropriate result is "I now stress truth."

Tuhba Wouldn't this be a great name for a city in Colorado? Tubha, CO—tobacco.

tumultuousness This is the word with the second most letters from the end of the alphabet. If there were such a word as "zzzzzzzzzzzz," that word would hold the record.

turdiform This word means "shaped like a thrush." Did you think otherwise? It is related to *turdus*, the Latin word for "thrush."

twang This word comes from the sound of a twang; it's onomatopoeic.

Ty Ty This isn't the name of an alcoholic beverage or the exclamation of someone watching Ty Cobb hit a home run. It is the name of a place in Georgia. Actually, the name should be Tied Tight. Supposedly a local tribe of Indians referred to the thick, twisted evergreen bushes there as "tied-tight bushes."

typewriter If you ever find yourself with a typewriter keyboard whose keys don't work except for the top row of letters (*qwertyuiop*), and if you need to type "typewriter," consider yourself fortunate. For "typewriter" is one of the longest words you can type without having to use any other keys.

U

ubiety This obscure word is actually the antonym of a very common word, "absence." It means "presence."

ugh This word comes from the sound of an ugh; it's ono-matopoeic. The word first appeared in print in 1765.

Ulgham You might never have guessed that the name of this city in the British Isles is pronounced "uffam."

Ulverston This British place-name is pronounced "ooston."

umpire This word ultimately comes from a word roughly equivalent to "non-pair." The idea is that an umpire is an un-biased third-party referee—in other words, he or she is not one of the pair of contestants, but a "non-pair." Say "a non-pair" a few times, and what do you get? "An onpair," or "an umpire." By the way, you can transpose the first and fourth letters of this word and come up with another word, "im-pure"!

un-come-at-able This real word with three hyphens means essentially what it says—unreachable.

---

unadorned   Scramble the letters of this word and the appropriate result is "and/or nude."

unau   The name of this animal is unusual in that it begins and ends with a *u.*

Uncertain   Exactly where do people in a state of uncertainty live? Could it be here in Uncertain, Texas?

unclean   This word is "pregnant" with twins: "uncle" and "an."

uncomplimentary   This may be the longest word in the English language that has one of each of the vowels, including *y,* all of them, except *y,* in reverse alphabetical order.

uncopyrightable   This is one of the longest English words with no repeated letters.

undergo   This word has a phantom antonym—a phantonym: "overcome," which isn't really an antonym of "undergo" but looks as if it could be.

underground   This word begins and ends with "und."

understudy   This word contains four consecutive letters in alphabetical order: *r, s, t,* and *u.*

ungarbed   Read the first part of this word backward (bragnu); then read the rest backward (de). Result: "brag nude."

uniformity   Let "uniformity" explain itself by simply moving its middle to the front: "I form unity."

united   The word "united" will no longer be united if you transpose its midsection. It will instead be the opposite of united—"untied."

Univac   The Univac computer takes its name from an acronym of "*univ*ersal *a*utomatic *c*omputer system."

unnoticeably   This is one of the longest English words, containing one of each of the vowels, including *y*, all of them, except *y*, in reverse alphabetical order.

unoriental   This word has all the vowels, each appearing only once and in reverse alphabetical order.

unsightly   Remove a few letters from this word and the appropriate result is "ugly."

untrustworthily   This is the word with the most letters from the end of the alphabet. If there were such a word as "zzzzzzzzzzzz," that word would hold the record.

untrustworthy   This is the word with the third most letters from the end of the alphabet.

untruthful   This is one of the longest words using only *u* for its vowel.

untumultuous   This is the word with the forth most letters from the end of the alphabet.

upholsterers   Scramble the letters of this word and the appropriate result is "restore plush."

upright   This word has a phantom antonym—a phantonym: "downright," which isn't really an antonym of "upright" but looks like it could be.

ushers This word can be split into two words: "us" and "hers." This word also has the rare distinction of being composed entirely of five personal pronouns in succession: "us," "she," "he," "her," and "hers."

Utahn You and I might believe a resident of Utah ought to be called a Utahan. But try to tell a Utahn that. In fact, Utahns are very protective of the spelling of their domonym.

Uttoxeter You might never have guessed that this British place-name is pronounced "uckster."

uturuncus This is one of the longest words using only *u* for its vowel. It's the name for sorcerers who supposedly turned themselves into jaguars.

uuula There are three *u*'s in a row in this early spelling of "uvula."

V

Vadis   As the story goes, the people who named this place in West Virginia wanted to name it after someone named Davis. But apparently they didn't want to be too obvious.

varsity   Not until 1846 was this word spelled "varsity." Since 1680, had been "versity." Can you guess how it was spelled before 1680? "University"!

vaudeville   This twentieth-century form of entertainment got its name from an Americanization of the French *vaux de ville,* the name of the valley (*vau*) of (*de*) Vire in Normandy.

Velcro   Although the name of this fabric fastener could have been derived from the English words "*velvet cro*chet," it comes, in fact, from the French equivalent, *velours* (velvet) *croché* (hooked). The name originated in the same country as the material, namely Switzerland, where it was invented by George de Mestral. Although the material may in certain respects resemble velvet, it is nylon. But "nylon" is another story (See "nylon," above).

vertigo   What we wonder about whenever we have free time on our hands?

vertuuus   This rare word has three *u*'s in a row. It's the four-teenth-century spelling of "virtuous."

vile   This word becomes "evil" if you move the *e* to the front.

viper   Vut you call the thing that vipes the vinshield?

virtuous   In 1933 a Hollywood studio banned this word from its films because it was considered "unsuitable"!

vitamin   When unexpected guests arrive at your door, vita-min for tea!

VOICES   This is the appropriate acronym for the Voice Oper-ated Identification Computer Entry System.

volunteers   Scramble the letters of this word and the appro-priate result is "never louts."

W

waggon This isn't exactly a misspelling of "wagon." It's the British spelling of the word.

waitress Scramble the letters of this word and the appropriate result is "a stew, sir?"

WARPATH This is the appropriate acronym for the World Association to Remove Prejudice Against The Handicapped.

Wassamassaw This is the phenomenal palindromic name of a swamp in South Carolina, located north of Charleston.

weeest Three *e*'s in a row! It means "littlest"; it's the superlative of "wee."

Weno The Canadian place-name Weno comes from a company motto: "We know." And that's the truth.

wheelbarrow This is one of the longest words beginning and ending with *w*.

whine This word comes from the sound of whining; it's onomatopoeic.

---

whippoorwill   This word comes from the sound that the whippoorwill, a bird, makes; it's onomatopoeic.

whiskey   Whiskey may be just water, unless you say it a certain way. It seems that in the eighteenth century, whiskey may have been spelled "whiskybea," from the Scottish Gaelic phrase *uisge beatha*, meaning "water of life." *Uisge* probably meant "water" (related to "aqua") and *beatha* appears to have meant "life" (as in "bio"). Thus if you drop the "bea" part of "whiskybea," you are left with the word for "water."

whisper   This word comes from the sound of a whisper; it's onomatopoeic.

whistle   This words comes from the sound of a whistle; it's onomatopoeic.

Why   "Why" is not always a question. It's also an Arizona place-name. The area is rather forbidding, and residents wondered why anyone would want to live there. So they named it Why.

Willy-with-the-wisp-and-Peggy-with-the-lantern   Here's a real word with eight hyphens! It's the name of a light appearing over a marsh at night.

window   The object of playing the lottery?

windshield   What shields the wind from oncoming cars?

word   This word is not only the word "word." It is also a word. Bet you've never thought about the word that way, have you? Well, okay, maybe you have. But have you ever thought of the word "word" as being autological? That's what it is. An autological word is a word that refers to what it denotes. So since the word "word" is indeed a word, it's autological. If you've followed that, you may want to check out the entry for "sentence" in this dictionary.

wordier   You can transpose the first and third letters of this word and come up with another word, "rowdier." Further, you can transpose the fourth and last letters of "wordier" and come up with "worried."

wppwrmwste   This word *could* be the longest English word with only one vowel. Actually, though, this is a fifteenth-century spelling of "uppermost."

Wymondham   The name of this town in Britain is pronounced "windum."

X

X   We all know of a famous person whose surname was *X* (Malcom X). But do we recall a famous person whose middle name was *S?* (See the *S* entry above.)

xylanthrax   Besides "Xerox" this is perhaps the only word that begins and ends with *x*. The word is an old name for "charcoal."

Y

yellow Virtually the same word that means "yellow" in Slovene means "red" in Czech; and the word meaning "yellow" in Welsh, means "blue" in Lithuanian; "yellow" in Hungarian means "red" in Latvian; "yellow" in Albanian means "green" in French; "yellow" in Low Latin means "blue" in Albanian. . . . It all depends how you look at it!

Yenruogis This is the name of a park in Iowa. And where in Iowa, you ask? . . . well, just read the word backward.

yippee This word comes from the sound of an exclamation of glee; it's onomatopoeic.

Yo Wouldn't this be a great name for a city in Delaware? Yo, Del.—yodel. Or for a city in Georgia? Yo, GA—yoga.

yo-yo There was a time when, strictly speaking, we could not have legitimately written "yo-yo" this way. The word was originally a company's registered trademark, a brand name, and therefore required a capital letter and, in some instances, a trademark symbol: Yo-Yo™.

Yorba Linda   This California place-name was created from the last name of an early settler, Bernardo Yorba, and part of the name of a nearby town, Olinda.

Ytterby   More chemical elements have taken their names from this word than any other word. Those elements are yttrium, terbium, erbium, and ytterbium. A Finnish chemist named Johan Gadolin discovered a rock in the tiny Swedish village of Ytterby. Apparently the rock contained all four of the elements.

Z

Zulu   Instead of coming near the end of the alphabet, this word could actually have begun with an *A*. For it originates from a Zulu chieftain named aZulu.

zyzzogeton   A three-*z* word! And one of the last words (alphabetically) you'll ever find. It denotes a genus of large South American leafhoppers. The "zyzzo" part probably comes from the sound that the zyzzogetons make. Now you know what a zyzzogeton sounds like—well, sort of.